# POEMS OF EVERYDAY LIFE

# Poems of Everyday Life

Danny L. Noss

Copyright © 2010 by Danny L. Noss.

ISBN:        Softcover            978-1-4568-3044-1

All rights reserved. No part of this book may be reproduced or transmitted in any form or by any means, electronic or mechanical, including photocopying, recording, or by any information storage and retrieval system, without permission in writing from the copyright owner.

This book was printed in the United States of America.

**To order additional copies of this book, contact:**
Xlibris Corporation
1-888-795-4274
www.Xlibris.com
Orders@Xlibris.com

# Contents

| | |
|---|---|
| 3 Going On 30 | 15 |
| 18 and Free | 16 |
| 215 Bonds | 17 |
| A Narcissist | 18 |
| A Real Bad Man | 19 |
| A Salesman's Mistake | 20 |
| A Slow Death | 21 |
| A Valet | 22 |
| Adultery Times Two | 23 |
| Agent Orange | 24 |
| Albert and Margaret | 26 |
| An Ants Life | 27 |
| Anasazi Indians | 28 |
| Angel on Earth | 29 |
| Apaches | 30 |
| Backhoe Operator | 31 |
| Bad Day | 32 |
| Baltimore Lady | 33 |
| Bees | 34 |
| Blaisdell Blue | 35 |
| Boyhood Memories | 36 |
| Broken Heart | 37 |
| Brothers | 38 |
| Bruce Huffer | 39 |
| Bruce's Friend | 40 |
| Buffaloes are Wild Animals | 41 |
| Business Today | 42 |
| Carrie Fitch (Down Syndrome) | 43 |
| Cat and Dog | 44 |
| Cats Life | 45 |

Cattle and Sheep ............................................................................ 46
Cheerleader .................................................................................... 47
Close Call ....................................................................................... 48
Coffee ............................................................................................ 49
College Bound ............................................................................... 50
College—Then and Now ................................................................ 51
Coralie Quintrall ............................................................................ 52
COSMO by Cosmo ......................................................................... 53
Coupons ......................................................................................... 54
Dan and Sandy ............................................................................... 55
David and Katie ............................................................................. 56
Day at the Beach ............................................................................ 57
Days Like This ............................................................................... 58
Death of a Pet ................................................................................ 59
Diamond ........................................................................................ 60
Divorce .......................................................................................... 61
Do As I Say, Not As I Do ............................................................... 62
Donner Island ................................................................................ 63
Dorothy ......................................................................................... 64
Dream Car ..................................................................................... 65
Easy Kill ......................................................................................... 66
Effects of Pain ................................................................................ 67
Ely, Nevada .................................................................................... 68
Email is Working Again ................................................................. 69
False Power .................................................................................... 70
Farm Life ....................................................................................... 71
Feelings of War .............................................................................. 72
Flying Eagle ................................................................................... 73
Full Circle ...................................................................................... 74
Full House ..................................................................................... 75
Gary and Kathy .............................................................................. 76
Gigolo ............................................................................................ 77
Gods People ................................................................................... 78
Golfing Lesson ............................................................................... 79
Good Programmer vs Poor Programmer ....................................... 80
Grandma's Apple Pie ..................................................................... 81
Graveyard Shift .............................................................................. 82
Grieving Process ............................................................................ 83

| | |
|---|---|
| Hands from God | 84 |
| Happy | 85 |
| Harold and Ethel Hall's 50th Wedding Anniversary | 86 |
| Hastie's Pest Control, Las Vegas, Nevada | 87 |
| Hatred | 88 |
| He Knew it was the End | 89 |
| He Tried | 90 |
| Healthy; Not | 91 |
| His Big Race | 92 |
| His First Birthday (Babies View) | 94 |
| Holocaust | 95 |
| How Many Cowboy Boots Are Enough | 96 |
| I Am Me | 97 |
| Improving Her Self Esteem | 98 |
| Indian's Point of View | 99 |
| Inspection Time | 100 |
| Invisible Moose | 101 |
| Janet's Fear | 102 |
| Joey | 103 |
| John Hambrick for Assembly | 104 |
| Key and Lock | 105 |
| Killing Morale | 106 |
| Laid Off | 107 |
| Las Vegas, Nevada Youth | 108 |
| Last Day | 109 |
| Life's Lesson | 110 |
| Life's Trials | 111 |
| Lost Calf | 112 |
| Lost Pay Check | 113 |
| Love from Afar | 114 |
| Lying Wannabees | 115 |
| Maiden 1, Vampire 0 | 116 |
| Main Gates | 117 |
| Mandy's First Snow | 118 |
| Mark the Brave | 119 |
| Marriage | 120 |
| Military Spouses | 121 |
| Moms | 122 |

| | |
|---|---|
| Money Does Not Buy Respect | 123 |
| Moving Blues | 124 |
| Moving Home | 125 |
| Mrs. Bach's Class | 126 |
| My Bear | 127 |
| My Cousins 409 | 128 |
| My First Car | 129 |
| My Friend Bert Fitch | 130 |
| My Friend from Town | 131 |
| My German Wine Fest Experience | 132 |
| My Racing History | 133 |
| My Spouse | 134 |
| Nancy | 135 |
| Natures Law | 136 |
| Never Happy | 137 |
| New Born Calf | 138 |
| New Computer | 139 |
| No Choice | 140 |
| No Thought | 141 |
| North Dakota | 142 |
| Ode to Leonard Chide | 143 |
| Off Limits | 144 |
| One Kings Place | 145 |
| Opening the Car Door | 146 |
| Our Mom | 147 |
| Outhouse and Pee Pot | 148 |
| Owning a Horse | 149 |
| Palm Trees | 150 |
| Perfect | 151 |
| Pontiac | 152 |
| Protecting My Home | 153 |
| Rattlesnake Roundup | 154 |
| Revenge | 155 |
| Rob and Nicole | 156 |
| Sawyer Fincher | 157 |
| Selma Sikes | 158 |
| Selma Sikes Birthday | 159 |
| Sexual Needs | 160 |

| | |
|---|---|
| Short | 161 |
| Short Pig Tale | 162 |
| Short Sale | 163 |
| Shorty | 164 |
| Single in 2010 (Male) | 165 |
| Sisters | 166 |
| Skin Deep | 167 |
| Sky Diving Experience | 168 |
| Sniper | 170 |
| Snow Skiing | 171 |
| Snowshoeing on Mount Charleston | 172 |
| South Dakota | 173 |
| Special Love | 174 |
| Strange Homecoming | 175 |
| Susan Bach | 176 |
| Tall | 177 |
| Tatonka (Buffalo) | 178 |
| Tattoos | 179 |
| The Ammo Dump | 180 |
| The Back Gate | 181 |
| The Boyfriend's View | 182 |
| The Buffalo Ranch | 183 |
| The Bus | 184 |
| The Camera | 185 |
| The Chair | 186 |
| The Church and the Devil | 187 |
| The Cold War | 188 |
| The Cowboys Winning Ride | 189 |
| A Dolphins Life | 190 |
| The Dream | 191 |
| The Early Adventures of Bogdan Jucan | 192 |
| The Elk Hunt | 193 |
| The Evil Sheep | 194 |
| The Family Farm | 195 |
| The Fawn and the Chipmunk | 196 |
| The Final Straw | 197 |
| The Flood | 198 |
| The Fly | 199 |

| | |
|---|---|
| The Hobo's Tale | 200 |
| The Hobo's Wife and Child | 201 |
| The Last Ten Feet | 202 |
| The Legacy of Reverend Law | 203 |
| The Meadow | 204 |
| The Mind | 205 |
| The Mission | 206 |
| The Old Man | 207 |
| The P.A.L.M. Process | 208 |
| The Peaceful Valley | 209 |
| The Peschongs | 210 |
| The Phone | 211 |
| The Poker Hand | 212 |
| The Slaughter House | 214 |
| The Song | 215 |
| The Stalker | 216 |
| The Stripper | 217 |
| The Suit from Hell | 218 |
| The Troll | 219 |
| The Wagon Train | 220 |
| The Wind | 222 |
| This Lady is Good | 223 |
| Those Few Seconds | 224 |
| Three Chihuahuas by Cosmo | 225 |
| Thrill of the Kill | 227 |
| Tim and Anna | 228 |
| Timothy Paul Curtin's Retirement | 229 |
| To Walk or Not | 231 |
| Tony and Connie Soliz | 232 |
| Training a New Officer | 233 |
| Tranquility | 234 |
| Tribute to Tobie (Golden Retriever) | 235 |
| Trip to Italy | 236 |
| True Friends | 237 |
| Trust | 238 |
| Turning Fifty | 239 |
| Two Illinois Ladies | 240 |
| Two Massacres | 241 |
| Two Shots | 243 |

| | |
|---|---|
| Uncle and Niece | 244 |
| Vegas Anger | 245 |
| White Man's Point of View | 246 |
| Who Is She | 247 |
| Who Is The Poor Man | 248 |
| Why Me | 249 |
| Work Environment | 250 |
| Working for the Rich | 251 |
| The End | 252 |

# Dedication

This book is dedicated to my wife Sandy who has put up with this Norwegian for over 35 years.

It is also dedicated to the many people who have given me the inspiration and material used to write some of these poems.

Two poems in this book have a special meaning to me. They are about Bert Fitch, a good friend who is giving cancer a hell of a fight and his daughter Carrie Fitch.

# 3 Going On 30

She was only three when her mommy came home that fateful day,
She wanted to see her mommy but the flag covered coffin was in the way.
She really did not comprehend when they said her mommy was gone,
How could she be gone when she was right here in the coffin on the lawn?
She cried when they would not open the cover,
All she wanted to do was to tell her mommy that she loved her.
At three she knew her mom was there,
She did not know the damage the IED had inflicted from somewhere.
She cried hard when she saw her mommy lowered into the ground,
She finally realized her mommy would no longer be around.
When she was ten her father talked to her about that fateful day,
Now it all made sense to her as he explained it in his special way.
Her pride in her mother's sacrifice took on a special meaning that day,
Her mother had given her life for what she believed in; in every way.
Every time she looked at her mother's picture on the wall,
She knew that when she was old enough she would also answer the call.
Now as she stands proud on the parade field in her Officer dress blues,
Her mother, watching from above knew that over the years she had received the clues.
She will stand proud where her mother stood,
She will carry on the proud tradition as she knew she would.

# 18 and Free

In the Army I will go,
It is time to do my own show.
I passed through Basic Training with ease,
Where I had my Advanced Individual Training a man could freeze.
Finally, schooling is over and it is time to run,
I am headed for Korea and it will be nothing but fun.
This is my first Army assignment and no parents around,
I am going to investigate the local bars and see what can be found.
There is a midnight to 4 AM curfew but it is OK if I do not go right away,
I can stay in the bar or become a bar girls yobo if I can pay.
Here the bar girls pick you up on the way to the door; you do not have to roam,
This is so much easier than trying to sway all the young girls back home.
Oh, Oh, what is wrong, why do I feel my private parts burn,
Hopefully at sick call they can give me penicillin and not be to stern.
After a few more trips to sick call over the next six months or so,
I am an old hat and know which medic for the penicillin I need to go.
I had a lot of fun during my tour in Korea, except for sick call,
I should have seen more country and not spent so much time at the Wall.
I just gave it away that this poem is from my past when I was 18 and free,
This special Wall is located in central Nuermberg, Germany you see.

# 215 Bonds

I walked into the bank one day,
I had 215 bonds to cash in some way.
I showed the stack of bonds to the young lady behind the table,
Her eyes got large as she thought, where is Mable?.
Mable usually did the bonds for this branch,
The young lady wished she could take a stance.
She knows the procedure for doing this,
To have Mable here to do it is her wish.
Ten, Twenty, Thirty minutes did fly by,
As she looked at the stack to go, she thought; me, why.
Her professionalism would not let her whine,
She smiled even though she knew it would take time.
Tick tock, tick tock, the clock did slowly pass,
She kept trudging along until she hit the last.
As she finished the last bond, she gave a sigh of glee,
From her monstrous task she was free.
As I a question or two did ask her,
Caused her to delay finishing, that is for sure.
The total value of the bonds is now in Black and White,
The condition of her fingertips is a fright.
Her dedication to her job and the customers is out of sight,
Ask anybody who she has helped; they will say that is right.
Everybody today has trials and tribulations in their life,
When working though she has to hide this strife.
Amanda at the Best Bank Branch is her name,
Professionalism and dedication to the customer no matter the task is her game.
Best Bank better appreciate employees like her,
She keeps customers coming back to Best for sure.

# A Narcissist

Somebody told me I was a narcissist the other day,
I was shocked and said "NO WAY".
Then I started to evaluate myself,
All the times I had to be first for the spotlight and the wealth.
When I worked on a project with a team, my name must go first,
Nobody better try to get in my way or I will for their blood thirst.
I always have to be in the spotlight that is the brightest,
I must always show that I am the mightiest.
My ideas are never wrong because I am always right,
Even if my ideas are proven wrong, it is not my fault they have blight.
I have the ability to convince people, I am right when I am wrong,
I hide behind my ignorance because I falsely believe I am strong.
I will do anything, right or wrong to stay on top,
I have no ethics or morals, for to win I will not stop.
If you try to take me down,
I will find a way to hurt you and not even frown.
I will never change from my narcissist ways,
I could care less when everybody else pays.

# A Real Bad Man

At six foot four inches tall and 220 pounds he was ready for any man,
He would start the night looking for anyone he can.
His habit was to pick the biggest man when he walked into the bar,
Usually he was the one who could walk back to the car.
He would swing first with all his might,
This would help him win the fight.
He had done this for so long,
He never thought about it being wrong.
A broken nose, jaw, arm or leg was normal for him,
His worst beating was from a guy named Slim.
As he got older the injuries became a bigger deal,
He was not feeling like such a big wheel.
He remembers one fight that was a tie,
They both ended up with broken legs; later they did not know why.
After fifty he started to slow down,
He wanted to make sure; for his kids he was still around.
He has been gone now for a long time,
His grave stone says "He never did whine."

# A Salesman's Mistake

This poem is about a salesman of the male kind,
Some of them see a female buyer and lose their mind.
We entered a dealer's lot looking to buy a car,
My wife would ask a question but never get far.
The salesman would look at me when he replied,
He would not look at my wife and she knew he lied,
Some salesmen always think the man is the boss of the house,
How many times do they have to lose a sale before they realize this is false,
When they answer my wife's question to me,
We turn and walk away and he loses his fee.

# A Slow Death

Everybody sees me drinking diet pop,
They all say "Why do you not stop".
I'm told that diet pop is pure poison for me,
I keep drinking it to see.
Morning, evening and night I drink it down,
I drink it no matter who I am around.
I am not saying it is safe to drink diet pop,
At least we will not get arrested if stopped by a cop.
I am sure that when the chemicals start to take over within me,
It will be the Lord saying it is time to pay my fee.
If the other diseases and ailments I have do not get me first,
The chemicals can then put me in a hearse.

# A Valet

There is a job that keeps you on the go,
It helps to be in shape so you can keep up with the flow.
With muscles bulging under their shirt and sexy legs they do their job,
One problem though is teaching them to fill out the log.
They have the speed of "Flash" and the flexibility of "Rubber Man",
They can leap one step in a single bound like "Superman"; yes they can.
They can get a good tip or an angry look,
They did not say anything about those looks in the Valet book.
They get to drive exotic cars some days,
To drive them for a few minutes is like a dream in many ways.
They get a bad reputation about abusing the cars,
They are the ones that before they go to work, hit the bars.
As usual a few make it bad for all,
When trouble comes they never seem to take the fall.
It is a job for the young; that is right,
When they retrieve a car, give them two seconds and they are out of sight.
With their tips they can make a fair amount of money,
As long as they do not call somebody's wife honey.

# Adultery Times Two

Two more beautiful people you will never see,
On their marriage day they were full of glee.
The years went by for them both,
Each one tried to show that they were the loving one most.
Neither knows who was the first to cheat,
They do know that he was the first to leave evidence on their sheets.
It did not take long for them to know,
That for each other there would be no more show.
They sat down to discuss what had happened between them,
They still feel like each other is a gem.
They still physically wanted each other,
They also wanted to have still others; oh brother.
They agreed that any trysts would be outside their home,
They would only use their home when they were both there alone.
They cared for each other a lot; but was not sure if it was love,
They needed more variety for their sexual needs to fit like a glove.
They knew that they could get a divorce some day,
For Income Tax purposes it was better to leave things this way.

# Agent Orange

The day I arrived in Viet Name the country gave me a shock,
Then I was assigned to the base camp in Da Nang and I knew I had a lock.
Working on helicopters did not seem so bad,
If I only knew then that later I would be sad.
The helicopters that sprayed Agent Orange also were sent to our shop,
Sometimes Agent Orange came off the choppers onto us, we could not make it stop.
Nobody said anything to us at the time,
They all told us that we would be just fine.
I made it through my tour and service obligation that year,
When I was reunited with my fiancée we both cried a lot of tears.
Our marriage was beautiful for us all,
The leaves were just starting to turn at that time of the fall.
We were walking on water when my wife was going to have a baby,
We decided we were going to call her Sadie.
Our world came crashing down when our daughter was stillborn that day,
It took a long time to get over how it happened that way,
With my wife's next pregnancy we were full of fear,
We lost our son also as his delivery date came near.
We asked ourselves; why is God punishing us so,
We prayed and prayed but it did not help us from being so low.

The third time my wife became pregnant we were scared as can be,
This time our son was born and we prayed to the Lord for our faith in thee.
The doctor told us one of his legs was deformed; we did not care,
He was alive and healthy so this we could bare.
The research we did told us the story of our children; those we lost and our new son,
The Agent Orange had created this grief and there was nowhere we could run.
Our next son was born healthy with ten fingers and ten toes,
We are now a family; happy and as bright and beautiful as a rose.
Ken's leg was amputated and he played sports in school with his new leg,
I wonder what the chance is he used it to drink from a keg.
Michael grew up as normal as anybody can be on this earth,
As parents we will always love them for all we are worth.

        This poem is dedicated to my friends Kenneth and Shirlene.

# Albert and Margaret

Albert came from the loins of the range,
But in Northwestern South Dakota that does not make you strange.
He grew into a man that is good with his hands,
He brought two special sons onto this land.
Margaret to Belle Fourche by way of Huron and Colony came,
Three daughters she did raise; who to three beautiful women did grow the same.
From other marriages did they both come,
They enjoyed each other's company and the beer, but please hold the rum.
Their love sprouted as time went on,
It continued to the point that it will never be gone.
Multiple grandchildren together they have brought to the table,
They will continue to play physical games with them as long as they are able.
From different directions they did come together,
But they will always share their love as one forever.
As this poem comes to a close,
They will get even with Dan for writing this prose.

# An Ants Life

Just because I am one of the smallest animals here,
They always try to kill me when I don't wear any protective gear.
Here comes another one,
Boy this isn't going to be fun.
Oh, he has such big feet,
When he steps on so many we lose a lot of meat.
Why does he always have to walk on our side,
When the sidewalk is so wide.
I can carry ten times my weight,
Is that why he always us hates.
Our cousin the Fire Ants are the bad boys,
Why do they always kick us around like toys.
Here comes another, it is good he is small,
Hurry everybody quick head for the wall.
We live in colonies some of the time,
Why when they always see us they whine.
When we quit running for our lives we have to pant,
Boy life is really a bitch as an Ant.

# Anasazi Indians

There is proof that the Anasazi were here at one time,
The structure of their housing makes them hard to climb.
They were intelligent and believed in the "other side",
If this is true I want to know if they survived the ride.
It is hard to believe that a whole Indian Nation disappeared from earth,
Unfortunately thieves have stolen many items for their worth.
Some of these items could explain parts of their past,
It is important because of the mystery of their nations last.
It is said that they all past through a portal in the kiev to the other side,
They were an Indian Nation of the strongest pride.
We will never know the truth about how they vanished,
Could it be that by some supernatural power they were banished.

# Angel on Earth

In this time of turmoil she is a silver lining,
She always thinks positive while everyone else is whining.
Every morning she prays to the Lord for peace in the world for all,
She knows this is a big task for the Lord when blocked by many walls.
She turns channels all day to see all the news,
With all the bad in the world the Lord cannot help but lose.
She knows this though it will never get her down,
She knows he cannot lose because he is above everybody on a mound.
Most people would give into unfaithful thoughts of the Lord,
But she will never doubt him for she does not listen to the hordes.
She knows he is her savior until her final day,
When it is time for her to go home, he will do it in his special way.
Her love for her faith will bring her through any troubles,
For Gods plan will also work for her husband with his stubble.

# Apaches

The Apaches were invisible in plain sight,
You always knew they were ready to fight.
They struck with the quickness of a snake,
They would with a knife across the throat rake.
Their enemies death was normally fast with taking their scalp very soon after,
Holding the scalp high they screamed with laughter.
When they desired, death could be slow,
The pain in the person's eyes would glow.
There are many ways that the Apaches could cause a person to die,
Others who have seen the results will agree this is no lie.
Whether by ant hill, leather strap or slowly losing their hide,
They knew this would be their last ride.
As with all Indian tribes the Apaches desire was to live in peace,
But the white man wanted to put them on a short leash.
When the white man pushed them to the brink,
In the Apaches desert home land they could the white man out think.
All Indians; as now, were a brave and proud people back when,
They counted many coups from other Indian tribes back then.
Outnumbered by the white man sealed their fate,
They were killed or put on a reservation at an alarming rate.
As the Apaches were forced to live the white man's way,
They were forced to learn their fighting techniques only at play.
All of the Apaches from that era are gone now,
Most of their knowledge the young people will never know how.
Today the young ones only know what they hear from their elders,
Some have had to leave the reservation to make a living as welders.
The Apaches as do all other Indian tribes strive to survive today,
Many are successful but the others try in any possible way.

# Backhoe Operator

His name is Gary Underhill,
Mastering the operation of the backhoe is his will.
The noise and power of the tractor gives him a thrill,
Until the day he has a headache and then he needs a pill.
He backs into place and drops the riggers,
He knows what he needs to do and calculates the figures.
With the riggers down and the back wheels high in the air,
His hands work the levers like a well greased pair.
The bucket reaches out and grabs the dirt like an extension of his hand,
With a special skill he changes the configuration of the land.
The bucket reaches out and cuts a perfect arch like a piece of fine art,
Working the bucket perfectly delays the need for new parts.
When the project is done with a precise cut in the ground,
Everybody was happy he had completed it while they were around.
The praise that Gary received was nothing new,
A day's work done; he knew it was time to have a brew.

# Bad Day

Today he was so mad at the world,
It affected him so that he hurled.
He remembered how good things used to be,
Now everyday he gets so mad he cannot see.
He is where he is now because of stupidity and greed,
Nobody will give him a chance when he knows he can still lead.
He has had to bring himself as low as he wants to go,
For most any job he will even go back to the snow.
He knows there are millions a lot worse off than he is,
But when he is asked about his life it is none of their bis.
His emotional state goes up and down,
Even some days it goes round and round.
His problem is that he trusted some people back then,
They acted friendly while deciding how to dump him when.
He knows that things will get better soon,
He also knows that next week a cow will jump over the moon.
He must find a way to dispel this anger before long,
He knows that he would never do anything wrong.
Keeping him going are his wife and his ability in himself to sell,
The ones that put him here can go to Hell.

# Baltimore Lady

Baltimore, Maryland is where she is from you see,
The Inner Harbor is where she used to be.
The Fish and Vegetable Market is a beautiful sight,
The Constitution was a mighty ship in a fight.
Now it sits in the Inner Harbor standing proud,
Ready daily to take on a large crowd.
A little south is Fort McHenry where the Star Spangled Banner was born,
Francis Scott Key wrote it as the sky with bomb blasts was adorned.
From the row houses to a place called Glen Burnie,
The distance from one to the other could be quite a lifestyle journey.
Las Vegas is where the author met this lovely lady,
She is beautiful and meticulous, nothing about her is shady.
She works the graveyard shift,
The author has never seen her miffed.
As with many people today, she desires to leave Las Vegas behind,
The decision is not as hard as it seems once you make up your mind.
The author wishes her in the future the best,
This special lady that the author feels is above the rest.
Michelle is her name,
Living a good clean life is her game.

# Bees

I am a bee says he,
I am a bee too says she.
We live in a hive said they,
We love to play in the hay.
Our family is very big,
Our hive is held up by a strong twig.
We love spring the best,
The purple flowers are better than the rest.
For our friend we produce honey,
We love making him money.
Our yellow and black bodies are beautiful and round,
Many places on earth we can be found.
We prefer not to sting when you come by,
So when we do sting; you ask why.
When we are scared that you might hurt us,
We sting to protect our hive by making quite a fuss.

# Blaisdell Blue

Blaisdell Blue gave a thrill to all,
Through the Rodeo season into the fall.
Blaisdell Blue was a roan as beautiful as the sky,
One look at him and you didn't have to ask why.
He was a large horse with lines that would impress,
His lines were tuned, but not to excess.
Blaisdell Blue lived up to his name,
Depositing cowboys on the ground was his game.
Blaisdell, North Dakota is where he performed the most,
Everybody came to see him as he was the host.
For many years he continued to put cowboys on the ground,
Round after round after round after round.
For a little boy of 10 to watch Blaisdell Blue was a dream,
It was better than having ice cream.
When the rodeo was over,
The young children would go home and try to ride rover.
The memories of watching Blaisdell Blue buck and kick for years,
Many times will bring joyous tears.
Blaisdell Blue has been long gone from this earth,
But every time he bucked the Rodeo fans received a lifetimes worth.

# Boyhood Memories

Danny was out on his great uncles farm one day,
There he hoped that he could long stay.
His great uncles farm was on the North Dakota plains,
Every year they prayed for more rain,
For Danny the things on the farm were fun,
He had plenty of space to run.
The cows, horses and chickens were a delight to him,
Especially when he rode the horse up to the hills rim.
Milking the cows had to be done twice a day,
Danny helped with the milking but in his own awkward way.
On the day they slaughtered chickens it was work for all,
One, Two, Three dozen chickens would get them through the fall,
Danny's job was to chase the chickens down,
With out their heads they can quickly run around.
Getting to the outhouse 200 feet from the house was quite a feat,
If you waited too long before finally getting there was not a treat.
When Danny drove the tractor he felt like a man,
The old John Deere went putt-putt-putt as it ran.
Pulling a wagon behind the tractor they would rocks into the wagon throw,
So that later in the year the crops would grow.
As he grew older Danny no longer went to the farm,
But every time he thinks about all the fun he had, he would feel all warm.

# Broken Heart

He loved her with all his heart and soul,
He would make diamonds from coal.
She is in his thoughts every minute of every day,
He would swim in a river of alligators if she on the other side would stay.
She told him she was his; but not all of her,
He bought her many presents including some of fur.
Their love making sessions were like animals from the wild,
When loving her, his touch was sensual and mild.
One day she said "I am not sure about us",
He gave her some space for he did not want to create a fuss.
His heart ached and his mind went crazy not knowing the cause,
She gave him the impression that she only wanted a pause.
He found out the pause was permanent when he saw her with another guy,
He searched his soul but could not figure out why.
They sent long emails back and forth for a while,
He tried his best but found it hard to smile.
He knew that if she changed her mind, he could not take her back,
He kept writing her emails, but they all ended up in the sack.
It took him a long time to get over her,
He finally realized he was over her for sure.
He moved on and eventually found true love that also loved him,
Life does go on even though you doubt that the chance is slim.

# Brothers

Brothers can be tight,
But one always thinks he is right.
Brothers normally get along in life,
Some can change though due to their wife.
As years go on some stay close and others drift apart,
In some families this can tear at the heart.
A brothers bond is special to all,
They will help each other; winter, spring, summer or fall.
There is a song verse that says it better than others,
"He is not heavy; he is my brother".

# Bruce Huffer

I have a very special friend named Bruce Huffer,
The Lord never made a man gentler or tougher.
Becky is the name of Bruce's beautiful loving wife,
She has given him three wonderful children in life.
Their everyday names are Sarah, Dan and Joe,
Their parents through not strict; did make them the line toe.
They are grown now, and creating their own lives,
Dan is married, but someday both boys will have wives.
Sarah is close to finishing College and then we know,
Onto living a successful and good life, she will go.
Bruce and Becky's faith in the Lord has always been strong,
When you walk hand-in-hand with the Lord, you can't go wrong.
Bruce was recently given some troubling medical news,
It is Prostate Cancer that is right now giving him the blues.
The diagnose is that it is in its early stages,
But only total recovery through family and friends minds rages.
Bruce's faith in the Lord will bring him through this with flying colors,
He can feel the love and prayers of family, friends and others.
This poem is a gift to Bruce from Dan Noss and maybe you've heard,
Who you can tell from this poem; is never at a loss for a word.

# Bruce's Friend

There is a man named Bruce,
Who has a good friend that is a little loose.
Bruce is always there to lend a friendly ear,
His friend even though loose, he does not need to fear.
His friend's actions, though sometimes hairy,
Gave him no reason that his friend should be scary.
With a good friend like Bruce by his side,
He knew that he would never lose his hide.
There is a man named Bruce,
Who has a good friend that is a little loose.

# Buffaloes are Wild Animals

Buffaloes are an integral part of the United States history today,
They are almost mystical from the stories people say.
They are still free to run wild in some of our parks,
People who forget they are wild are easy marks.
People who do not pay attention,
Are those usually a sleep when the wild part is mentioned.
Buffalo are graceful and very fast,
If one puts its sight on you, you will never last.
Buffalo are beautiful on their natural range,
Some ranches give tours if you want to part with some change.
I know of a Buffalo Ranch in South Dakota that they call home,
It is on land where the Sioux Indians used to roam.
To drive into the herd is quite a thrill,
Up your spine it gives you a chill.
To be so close to them that way,
Always makes it a very special day.
The ranch owners who run the herds,
Will be the first to tell you these words.
They respect the Buffalo every day,
For they are wild animals and can hurt or kill you many ways.

## Business Today

It is hard to work in today's society and be happy,
You would like to enjoy your work and be snappy.
But greed overtakes honesty everywhere,
Whether it is a service contract or a physical chair.
People have to work in bad situations because of kickbacks,
Because other people morals lack.
The corruption in our society starts at the top,
Bribery is in the open by Congress and must stop,
The small businesses see Congress flaunting illegal actions,
They say we might as will be part of those factions.
It took the last 65 years to get this way,
It will not start to change until we make the criminals pay.

# Carrie Fitch (Down Syndrome)

Some people look at Down Syndrome individuals as not normal,
These people lose a lot in life because they think of themselves as more formal.
A young lady who is the daughter of my good friends is loving, caring and smart,
Like her parents, I love her with all my heart.
They say that Down Syndrome individuals do not have a temper or are not strong,
I do not know who first said this, but they are wrong.
When given the chance they can accomplish major tasks,
If you do not believe me you can their parents ask.
They can beat many people in sports, video games and love,
They are so caring they would not hurt a morning dove.
She calls me Uncle and I call her Niece,
She would give you the last of her chocolate piece.
I might embarrass her with this line about when she soiled her clothes,
One day as I watched her; it looked like pea soup and ran from her back to her toes.
She was six months old so she will not remember this,
Let me tell you; for me it was not bliss.
She is in her 30's now and working most every day,
She brings love and happiness to everybody in many ways.
Her name is Carrie Fitch and she is proud of herself as she should be,
Her parents worked with her as she turned into a beautiful young lady you see.

# Cat and Dog

The cat would not take it eyes off the dogs head,
The dog starred back but his head was starting to feel like lead.
This standoff had been going on for a long time,
They were both so still they could be a mime.
They both knew that the first one to move was in trouble,
The other one would chase them across the rubble.
A squirrel running by woke them out of their trance,
They both chased the squirrel in what looked like a dance.
After the squirrel ran up a tree,
They both realized that from the trance they were free.
They starred at each other again and said what the heck,
The starring was giving them both a stiff neck.
They both decided they would head for home,
Until the next time they would roam.

# Cats Life

My human thinks she owns me; NOT,
Before that happens she will be dead and starting to rot.
When my litter box is not cleaned just right,
She does not realize how I can fight.
When I sit on her lap and extend my claws,
I'm getting back at her for trimming the dogs paws.
When she is home, all her attention is supposed to be mine,
It is that dang dog that causes her to drink too much wine.
She knows better than to bring me the wrong food,
When I need to be I can be pretty rude.
When she comes home I need to show her I am the boss,
I run to her and then walk away; it is her lose.
When she goes to bed she has to be nice to me,
I sleep under the covers by her knee.
If in the night she kicks me in the face,
I give her a little nip and you would link she was in a race.
I know she will outlive me by years,
But I know when that happens she will be full of tears.

# Cattle and Sheep

Cattle in Spring Valley did graze,
Sheep in Ruby Valley did their young raise.
Tension between the cattlemen and sheepherders seems to always last,
Even though the land they both use is vast.
They both want the pasture with the tallest grass,
Normally it is settled with a rifle blast.
As time went on; they found out they could exist together,
What helped make this decision was the rainy weather.
The grass grew back very fast,
The taller it grows the longer it will last.
Over time the rifles became silent for all,
Understanding and knowledge helped bring down the wall.
Now through range rotation, the grass sustains the cattle and the sheep,
But with both of them using the same pastures the manure sure gets deep.

# Cheerleader

This is Jane's first year to try to be a cheerleader at school,
I knew if she did not make it; she would be blue.
She had practiced a lot the last two years,
Many days her sore arms and legs brought her to tears.
Her mother was a cheerleader in High School and College every year,
Her mother is her coach and taught her many cheers.
The first day of tryouts was hard to bear,
At times she felt like pulling out her hair.
Every morning she was almost too sore to walk,
It even hurt when she tried to talk.
She knew without the years of practice it would be worse,
At this point in the tryouts she would have needed a nurse.
Things got a lot easier near the end,
She also had made many new friends.
The day the list came out she was both happy and sad,
The news for her was good but for many of her friends it was bad.
She was also a cheerleader every year through her High School and College time,
Now as a mother she hopes her daughter will follow in her steps and really shine.

# Close Call

The cars blinker said right,
Then it turned to the left tight.
As the car slowed to turn,
I decided to go around it with a slow burn.
As I went by I looked at the driver in shock,
The driver was using a knife trying to open the handcuff's lock.
I dialed 911 and relayed my story,
They told me to stay away from that vehicle or I could be sorry.
After another block I met three police cars,
On the news later I found out the driver was behind bars.
He was guilty of many crimes,
Including killing somebody for a dime.
I learned a valuable lesson that night,
Letting your anger rule your thoughts is never right.
That night when I went to bed,
I hugged my children tight and caressed their heads.
The next time I see a person driving bad,
I will stay calm for if I am hurt; I do not want my family to feel sad.

# COFFEE

Coffee is a drink that most people want,
For people who cannot drink it, others will taunt.
Some drink it straight up black,
Others will drink it while laying in the sack.
Some will drink a little with their sugar and cream,
All the sugar and cream will give their clothes a tight seam.
There are now more flavors than countries on earth,
People will quickly drink it for all they are worth.
Do not ask a non-drinker to make some for you,
For they know not what they do.
Your first drink might be your last,
If you do not get rid of it all real fast.
People who drink too much booze,
Feel that coffee will help them their hangover lose.
Coffee in Germany and Italy will hold up a spoon,
Drinking too much of it can make you crazy as a loon.
People drink coffee in many different ways,
My great uncle moved his from the cup to the saucer to cooler stay.
My friend in Korea drank it with cognac in it,
He could drink all night and still be fit.
People will be drinking coffee until the end of the earth,
They will enjoy it until then for all it is worth.

# College Bound

Her last day of High School her head was in the sky,
She was glad High School was over, but missing her friends made her cry.
The preparation for college during the summer was a chore,
She knew now that everything she had heard was not lore.
She got her books, computer and was assigned to a dorm room,
With the dorm cleaning required, she was glad she learned how to use a broom.
The first couple of nights in the dorm,
She wished she was home because of the storm.
She received her class schedule and her eyes got big at first,
She started rating them from best to worst.
The boys were older and pretty brash to the girls,
Some of them were so gross she wanted to hurl.
She knew her classes were more important than anything else,
Her main objective was to finish college and accumulate some wealth.
She knew that she would do just fine,
She has high values and knows how to tell somebody they crossed the line.

# College—Then and Now

I quit High School two days into my senior year,
I was 17 and knew it all; I had nothing to fear.
I joined the U.S. Army a year later after not accomplishing much of anything,
I was still not ready to hear any classroom bells ring.
I eventually took the G.E.D. exam with a passing score,
You could hear everyone in my class of one (me) roar.
In 1975 I took my first college class,
It was fun and I even passed.
Each time I moved, I would more college classes take,
At that time I did not realize what was at stake.
24 years later after attending seven different colleges around this earth,
I received my Associate of Arts degree and the benefits of its worth.
I took a few more classes from another college school,
Obtaining 106 semester hours from eight colleges might seem like a fool.
I also received 69 semester hours from A.C.E. for my military skills,
I worked hard for those semester hours and did not take any pills.
With my 175 semester hours and Associate of Arts degree, I decided to take on the world,
The brick wall I ran into hurt so bad I could have hurled.
When you are 58 years old with 38 years of experience and no advanced degree,
The 2010 employment search can quickly make you feel like history.
Parents, if your child can only do it this way; then be it,
But if they can go to college, make them for four to six years there sit.
If I could do it over again I would not change a thing,
For young people starting out, you need a more college type structure to this world bring.

# Coralie Quintrall

There was a lady named Coralie,
Who loved life so dearly.
She did her own thing each day,
But always in her special way.
Her children though spread a wide,
Some were close and some were far, but they all cried.
When the Lord unexpectedly decided to bring her home,
He decided he needed her more than when she lived alone.
She touched the lives of many with love,
She will continue to do so from high above.
She is physically gone from our sight,
But our loving memories of her will always be right.
Each of us will have our special memories to carry along,
Whenever these memories pass through our mind, we can never go wrong.
Coralie was a mother, aunt and grandmother to everybody she met each day,
She became instantly special to them in many ways.
She was always there to love with all her might,
That love will continue to grow in us as she sits on the Lord's right.
This poem was written for you by your adopted son Dan,
Who by knowing you will always be a better man.

# COSMO by Cosmo

I am almost 14 years old now and do not feel so well,
By the looks on mom and dad's faces they can also tell.
The veterinary doctor told them my heart is bad,
I know it is not good because their faces are sad.
Aunt Sandy is here but I feel too bad to get up,
Mom and dad are holding me like when I was a pup.
I am riding in Aunt Sandy's car; I do not know where we go,
I feel worse; I wish my blood would faster to my heart flow.
We are at Aunt Sandy's house now,
I can breathe a little better, but how.
I can hear everybody in the other room,
I feel so bad I can see my dog angels who over me loom.
Oh, why is the pain so bad in my chest?,
I have to let out a loud yelp, then maybe I can rest.
Who is that picking me up; oh it is Uncle Dan,
I am glad he is here with the warmth of his hand.
My heart hurts so and it is getting harder to see,
I can feel his hand rubbing my back as sensual as can be.
The pain is subsiding and my breathing is slower,
There is no more pain and . . . .

## Eulogy

Cosmo gave unconditional love for almost 14 years,
She is gone now, but we will always remember her through our tears.

## Coupons

Coupons can become a lifestyle,
They have been around for a long while.
It is a way to entice you to buy,
Everything from milk to what you can fry.
You can spend hours looking in newspapers and magazine ads,
Compiling the information can take many note pads.
A lady of today uses a computer and scanner,
This information is sorted by a program that gives her result in any manner.
It is a fact that initially coupons save you money,
The husband asked his wife "How many hours do you spend on coupons honey".
He said "If you add your time at minimum wage what is the actual cost",
He knew he had said the wrong thing when he could see her look of frost.
From that day on he enjoyed the fruits of using coupons every day,
It took him a while to get on his wife's good side; by the way.

# Dan and Sandy

Dan and Sandy sitting in a tree,
Enjoying life in the land of the free.
The tree met their desires just fine,
Even allowing some cruises and wine.
Then the big bad woodcutter came along,
He said their tree was too good, and that was wrong.
He said it was time to bring them back to earth,
Let them soul search the value of their worth.
He started removing slices of the tree starting at the base,
Bringing them to the realization of this rat race.
As the slices kept falling out and the tree got shorter,
They pulled together and opened the bags of mortar.
With the mortar around the tree firmly in place,
The woodcutters saw could not keep the pace.
The tree was now stabilized and refused to be shortened anymore,
Dan and Sandy had decided to make a stand and let out a roar.
They knew that everything would eventually come out right,
Their love for each other will always give them the will to fight.
Most poems have an ending but this one not,
One thing will never change; that Sandy is HOT!!

# David and Katie

Woody and Susan raised two beautiful daughters,
Katie and Nicole up north by the Lake Michigan waters.
The Lord took Woody home to be by his side,
Before he could see his daughter Katie taken as a bride.
Their dogs Romeo and Leonardis bring them love and enjoyment,
A Labrador and a Mastif can require steady employment.
With the job market in the Milwaukee area in the dumps,
David and Katie changed direction to smooth out the bumps.
David enlisted in the U.S. Army at 26 for Military Training,
Their life turned to sunshine instead of raining.
David left for Basic and Advanced Training one day,
Katie found out soon after that she was in a motherly way.
Estella Maria was the name chosen for their lovely daughter,
Susan; who as a brand new grandmother was walking on water.
David's first assignment as a soldier will be Pusan, South Korea,
Hey, how about that; his first assignment rhymes with Estella Maria.
David's off-duty time includes Katie, Estella Maria and his guitar,
Do not question him on this, no matter who you are.
This poem was written by a friend; Dan Noss for a gift,
Who wishes both of them the best in life without a rift.

# Day at the Beach

The sun shown bright on their faces as they walked to the car,
The moon still showed itself like an aging star.
The family was going to spend the day at the beach,
When they arrived at the beach the children for their towels did reach.
They all found a place on the sand to rest,
They all ran towards the water for the temperature to test.
They swam and played in the ocean for quite a while,
The young ladies straightened out their bathing suits they bought to be in style.
They lay in the sun for a while before they headed home,
In the car the young ladies were looking for a comb.
At home they showered and settled down for the night,
In their sleepwear they decided which movie to watch that was just right.
As they all got up and headed for bed,
They all agreed that the day was the best; enough said.

# Days Like This

I came to work today, my sixth day in a row,
Tomorrow is my day off; my face is a glow.
It didn't take long to know things were bad,
The way I performed my duties was sad.
I had to check people through the gate,
Then call security in the lobby at a fast rate.
This should be very easy to do,
But I kept forgetting to call and say who.
The more cars I miss the angrier I became,
All I need now is for it to rain.
I'm at lunch now trying to relax,
I hope in the next four hours I get the right facts.
I'm 50 minutes into the second half,
So far I don't need to be saved by a raft.
Things should go smooth for the rest of this shift,
If not, my supervisor will use his foot to give me a lift.

# Death of a Pet

Some people say that pets are just dogs or cats,
Some people love to have a pet like a rat.
Most people with pets will say they are part of the family to,
When one of them is sick the whole family is blue.
Pets bring many things to a family including joy,
Some male pets get so large they call them "Big Boy".
It does not matter if you are young or old,
You go into a panic when your pet gets a cold.
They will give you their undivided love all the time,
When you are happy, sad, grumpy or fine they can read any sign.
Most pets last about 15 human years,
When it is time for them to go many people are full of tears.
There are many ways to remember your pets,
In a cemetery, an urn or have them preserved and standing by the steps.
Pets will be here as long as humans; which is forever,
Pet lovers will not ever be without them; never.

# Diamond

A diamond first appears in the rough as coal,
Then it is compressed in the earth's soul.
As it grows older it is shaped into a beautiful perfect gem,
The gem part also pertains to a young lady who is like roses with perfect stems.
She is different than most young people these days,
She is responsible and more mature in many ways.
Her love of family, work and country are never in doubt,
The path she has chosen for her life is a straight route.
She is a valued member of the National Guard for her state,
I know that everything she does is first rate.
Her appearance is impeccable every day,
She takes pride in everything she does and completes tasks the perfect way.
Her intellect is second to none,
She picks up complicated processes on the run.
When times are tough for her family, she can always be found,
She has made sacrifices to ensure they are safe and sound.
I could lie and say that her name is Lyman,
The young lady's name this poem is about is Diamond.

# Divorce

Divorce is more than a seven letter word today,
Too many people are using it to get out of marriage the easy way.
Two people say they cannot live together any more,
They never say the real reason which comes from their core.
Many people only think of themselves when they want out,
Then there are the people that get mad and only want to shout.
More divorces are because of cheating on the mother by the father,
Sometimes they want to get caught, then act like it does not bother.
It always makes it harder when there are kids,
When they argue they need to not flip their lids.
It is always bad when one parent uses the kids against the other,
Emotionally it is worse for the father to turn them against the mother.
Divorce is never good for the involvement of all,
It causes more people than just the husband and wife to fall.
If a couple cannot work things through,
Than it is normally because one or both broke the Golden Rule.

# Do As I Say, Not As I Do

There are people in this world that live by double standards every day,
Most are in management where they affect people in a negative way.
They say you cannot do this or that,
But everybody notices they do it themselves; what a rat.
They think because they are management, it does not pertain to them in any way,
Then they use those things to discipline people who always seem to pay.
Companies can lose good people when this happens to them,
They usually lose them at a critical time, but never know when.
Staff will never tell a manager what they do,
If they do, their co-workers would call them a fool.
I do know of what I speak,
For I have worked for many a geek.
If the workers do not quit, they can group together as one,
When they do that, for their manager it is not fun.
Sometimes, that is what it takes before some people can see,
They must change their ways or pay a heavy fee.

# Donner Island

The five men washed up on the island in June,
After floating about the ocean for two weeks they were crazy as a loon.
They had been out of food and drink for a week,
They used what strength they had for food and drink to seek.
They found very little to sustain them as they got weak,
They knew that death was coming to all; they cried as they were meek.
They knew now what went through the Donner parties minds,
Their physical conditions were close to the same kind.
As the days passed and they knew that they could no longer sustain,
They agreed it would not matter who was the last to remain.
They decided to cut five sticks of different lengths,
They knew that to fulfill this agreement would take all their strength.
When each mans time would come,
Suicide would be the way it would be done.
The first person to go was the hardest,
It did not matter that he was the smartest.
The thought of eating his parts,
Made them soul search from their hearts.
They finally succumbed to reality and started to eat,
They tried their best to not think that this was human meat.
Three more followed suit until there was only one,
He knew it was only time before he was also done.
Strangely his dilemma at this time; was follow suit and use suicide as an out,
Or die a painful death by starvation this was no doubt.
Two years later when a yacht stopped by the island they found bones,
But never knew the truth about these five men all alone.

# Dorothy

She was well known around Randall,
She was quite a woman to handle.
She had a daughter with her husband Mac,
Daughter Jeri became a beautiful lady, which is a fact.
She had a very thick crust, which when broken showed a soft core,
If you could not break the crust, you could be headed for war.
From day one I felt that I was one of the few,
That was accepted into her secret society crew.
She worked for years at Magee's grocery store without making a scene,
Later her scheduled morning Café visit with friends was routine.
She would get mad with a whisker rub, but you could not be weak,
Every time I saw her I would give her a whisker rub across her cheek.
She would grumble and say how much better I would look without it,
I would smile and do it again knowing it would put her in a fit.
Even though she was hard to get close to; sadly she is gone from us now,
We all miss her grumpy voice and that sly smile; and how.
I will continue to show her my love every once in a while,
By whisker rubbing her grave stone with a loving style.
Dorothy "Dot" Michalek of Randall, Minnesota was her name,
Making people think she was gruff all the time was her game.

# Dream Car

My dream car has always been a 1956 Cadillac Hearse,
Do not laugh some people have done worse.
My car is black as a moonless night,
Except for the red, orange and yellow flames that show bright.
The 426 Hemi is full of chrome, the supercharger is sticking out of the hood,
The car looked like it could scream; and it would.
It has small Mickey Thompsons on the front and Mickey Thompson slicks on the back,
Hooker headers, Thrush mufflers and Hurst shifter; there is not much it lacks.
To make it drivable on the highway, 3.89 rear gears pushed it from the rear,
As it goes down the street, it is followed by cheers.
The interior is made of the best leather,
The down mattress in the back is light as a feather.
The inside walls and front headliner are tuck and rolled,
The headliner in the back; that is one large mirror where everything shows.
I went to sleep many nights thinking about this car,
This car never became real, but it will always be my star.

# Easy Kill

The mountain lion had not eaten for days,
She was so hungry she looked at things through a haze.
She knew if she did not find fresh meat before long,
Her unborn cubs would die or the birth could go wrong.
Samuel packed quickly as he left the house,
He made sure that he was as quiet as a mouse.
His mother told him he should not do something he knew he could,
He was still mad at his mother when he entered the woods.
He was brave until the woods turned dark,
As a ten year old, he now thought he should not have done this on a lark.
He was too far to go home,
He unrolled his mattress of foam.
The mountain lion picked up the scent at dawn,
She was glad that to get a meal she did not have to go on a lawn.
She saw him and noticed he was small and slim,
There would be less meat but an easy win.
He sensed something was wrong,
Then he saw her on the ground.
They both froze in place,
He knew he could not win a race.
He swung his hatchet to try and scare her off,
She jumped on a limb to get more loft.
As he moved closer she sprang landing on his head,
He let out a scream as his blood ran red.
He tried to swing the hatchet while fighting back the pain,
Drops fell on them as it started to rain.
The boy tried to scream but no sound came out,
The boy had lost this life ending bout.
The mountain lion quickly satisfied her appetite until she was full,
She then moved and covered him which was a heavy pull.
The young boy's final thought came about the same time his mother awoke at home,
"I Love You mom and I am sorry about leaving you alone."

# Effects of Pain

The pain was intense and the pills helped out,
Without the pills you want to shout.
When the cause of the pain is stopped you are glad,
But later the effects of the pills on you can make you mad.
Things that were not a problem before,
Now give you some trouble and hits you to the core.
You try to ensure that you slow down to do it right,
But you still make small mistakes that cause an internal fight.
Who knows what the end result will be,
I guess you just have to suck it up and later see.

# Ely, Nevada

There is a town in Nevada named Ely (E-le),
It has a strange effect on many people; really.
It is 250 miles to any larger city,
But that is not a reason to give its residents pity.
Ely has many things that make it good,
With the mountains and trees you are surrounded by wood.
The altitude of 6,500 feet makes the air with no pollutants clear,
When you go up into the mountains, you have a little to fear.
Vehicle trouble, weather and wild animals are a few,
If you are from a big city you will not have a clue.
The weather in Ely is the best in all seasons,
The year around temperatures gives you to go there a good reason.
Riding the old steam locomotive Engine # 93 is quite a thrill,
The cost of the ride is not a big bill.
You go through a tunnel; the sight of a bad wreck years ago,
John Mariani was instrumental in salvaging the train while others watched the show.
Cave Lake, Comins Lake and Illipah Reservoir are nearby lakes with bountiful fish,
You can catch your limit whenever you wish.
Driving over Kalamazoo pass is a beautiful sight,
You cannot cross it because of snow until July; that is right.
The largest copper mine at one time is a few miles away in Ruth,
Yes sir; there is documentation that makes this the truth.
US Highways 93, 50 and 6 cross each other in this place,
Ely is also the gathering location for two international road races driven with grace.
If you ever drive the Loneliest Highway in America (US 50) you must stop in Ely,
You will never forget your stay there; really.

# Email is Working Again

The school year started with a bang,
Then the email devil rang.
You could not send email to parents.net,
It was as bad as you thought it could get.
The parents wanting to know,
Why your email will not go.
The office personnel were the same,
But the email devil proved hard to tame.
Then on a bright day in December,
Came an early Christmas present to remember.
An email from Mr. Noss,
That we are no longer at an email lose.
Christmas is a time of joy,
Parents are receiving email again, oh boy.

# False Power

Every organization has someone,
Who likes to take away everybody's fun.
They have a position in the middle of the deck,
They try to make others lives a wreck.
They have perceived power in their own mind,
When in fact their false power makes them blind.
They push people's buttons until they are brought down to earth,
Then the reality hits them of exactly what they are worth.
They will get away with only what people will let them do,
Even after being put in their place, they want to wear bigger shoes.
They are tolerated by others but not really liked,
At the company picnic they usually will the punch spike.
Life would be simpler if they moved on,
But they will not because they are a very good con.

# Farm Life

The pig fell in the mud,
The cow chewed his cud.
The chicken an egg laid,
The egg a chick made.
The bull went looking for a cow,
The boar went looking for a sow.
The piglet had a curly little tail,
The dog followed the farmer to get the mail.
The sheep fell sound asleep,
The puppy found a bone to keep.
The horse was running fast,
The donkey always came in last.
The farmer's wife baked many things,
The farmer's daughter hopes for a wedding ring.
The farmer's first son heads to the bar,
The farmer's second son cannot wait to get his first car.
The cats are in the barn all day,
The kittens play in the hay.
The mice eat in the bin of grain,
While crops in the field prayed for rain.
This about covers all things on a farm,
If I missed one or two do not be alarmed.

# Feelings of War

War is never fun,
When you have to live or die by the gun.
You knew what lay ahead when you signed on,
But the reality does not sink in until a comrade is gone.
At this point your instincts turn on,
You are glad for the training you hated, and that the knowledge is not gone.
When the enemy prefers to be a martyr over life,
You have to react before you think; if you want to again see your wife.
They say you cannot think of death,
Your mind says you have to; to ensure you can take another breath.
The gore of war can affect your mind in different ways,
It is not a thing that just goes away; as some people say.
Blood and guts are not everything there is about war,
Humanitarian jesters by the military can do a lot more to touch the core.
The love of your family and the gratitude of your country; keeps you moving on,
When engaging the enemy, thoughts of your family and country are long gone,
Training and instinct are what will keep you alive at that moment in time,
Working together as a well oiled team will keep you fine.
If you are wounded and have to go home,
Your emotions run happy and sad as you think of your team; when you are alone.
When back in the country that you love,
Your family is with you and you honor your comrades by praying to the Lord above.

# Flying Eagle

Spotted Horse looked out at his son Flying Eagle at play,
It is time to give him his horse that is gray.
He must learn to ride him bareback and without holding on to the mane,
He would need to learn to ride like this even in the rain.
The first day he worked on staying on while holding onto the mane very tight,
Spotted Horse was very proud of him for he did most things right.
Learning to ride well could save his life,
Flying Eagle also had to learn how to use a knife.
With a horse he could travel fast but the knife could save him night or day,
To win a fight to the death he must know how to use a knife in many ways.
Flying Eagle learned fast and shortly he was one of the best,
When it came to proving himself he passed the test.
The day that Tatonka was spotted the training became real,
Riding into the herd while using a lance and not being killed is quite a deal.
After the hunt Spotted Horse searched everywhere for his son,
Then he saw him coming towards him at a full run.
He couldn't wait to tell his father how Tatonka had fallen under his lances weight,
He will never forget the sight when his lance struck as it went in straight.
Spotted Horse could not hold back his pride as his yell carried across the sky,
Flying Eagle's first hunt and the Eagle feather he received made him want to fly.

# Full Circle

The sky is blue,
The airplane flew.
It cut through the air,
Below you could see the fair.
At the fair there were fun rides,
The ocean next to the fair was at high tide.
In the ocean there are many fish,
To catch his limit is the fisherman's wish.
The fisherman's boat was his home,
From there he usually did not roam.
One day to the big city did the fisherman go,
After five years he still has nothing to show.
The fisherman was on a flight with the movie ready to start,
He looked down at the fair and it excited his heart.
This poem shows how the world goes around,
When you really look at what can be found.

# Full House

After years of struggling, I finally bought my house,
It was pretty big and so quiet you could hear a mouse.
Life was good until one day when the door bell rang,
When I opened it the sight hit me with a bang.
My brother, his wife and two kids without a place to live,
I could not say no, so I said come in; a roof I can give.
Hiding on the side was their dog and cat,
The dog growled at me and cat was very fat.
They said they lost their jobs and house the other day,
I told them they could stay, but they needed to look for another way.
Two weeks later as they were settling in place,
I opened the door again to see my niece's face.
With tears in her eyes and a boyfriend standing behind,
The disheveled look of them about made me blind.
Her mother told her they could not stay,
They were lazy and in the way.
My nice big quiet home became a mess,
Do not get me wrong, I did not think of them any less.
When it comes to relatives, you cannot chase them away,
You only wish they could get jobs to help you pay.
The economy right now is in the dumps,
Almost everybody is ending up taking their lumps.
I guess this is what life will be,
Because family is family you see.

# Gary and Kathy

Gary, what an eager beaver; ambition he does not lack,
Kathy, so nice you would never give her back.
Together they make two into one,
Their love for each other makes it even that much more fun.
From Pennsylvania by way of Utah to Ely did Gary stop,
Kathy, a Las Vegas lady when to Ely she came made many hearts hop.
As with all families in this day and age,
Their children find ways to put them in a rage.
Their devoted love for their children sometimes is in a haze,
But children will be children and hopefully they will change one of these days.
Their love and caring for each other will pass the test of time,
Boy; isn't it hard to make every verse in this poem rhyme.
Lest we forget their special children, 1 cat and 3 dogs,
Could you imagine the household if they also had some pet hogs.
Their friendship and support to Dan and Sandy will a lifetime run,
When it is their time to reach the pearly gates they will already have won.
They will eventually ride together through heaven where it is so ruhig (quiet),
In their brand new old fashioned Buick.

# GIGOLO

If it walks and is of the female gender, it is on his list,
His attractiveness turns them into putty when he does insist.
Some were one nighters while others stayed around longer,
As the numbers on the list grew, he kept getting stronger.
Every night they run to him like honey,
He works two jobs to keep them happy with sex and money.
His quest to conquer all nationalities is always on his mind,
A conquest from Brazil and Argentina are the next to find.
He was serious about one until her true colors came out,
After that, all he thinks about is more quests and beer that is stout.
He normally tries for one a night,
If the opportunity arises, two in one night is by him alright.
One night he met his match with a tigress, who tore him apart,
He was sore in so many places including his ass cheeks he could hardly fart.
She perforated his right nipple and left teeth marks on his ass cheek,
His back looks like a road map with nail marks that made him feel meek.
One time, two times, three and more,
She wanted to keep going until his member was raw to the core.
He knew he had taken a wild ride,
He did not know to what extent until he saw of the condition of his hide.
Being sore did not slow him down,
Within a fortnight he had one from Brazil found.
At his young age the conquests are fun,
As long as he makes sure he does not from a husband have to run.
As the years go by his sexual escapades will be for emotions instead of conquests; NOT,
As long as he insures he does not catch something that makes his member rot.

# Gods People

People always say,
Why will he let things happen that way.
They think his love for them is unreal,
If they do not keep praying it is no big deal.
There are those that Church is not their thing,
But their lifestyle makes all the right bells ring.
There are also those that attend Church many times a week,
They do not ring any bells but brag on their Church going streak.
Some people think that all the disasters is a way to test their faith in him,
But he knows that this being the reason for them is very slim.
All the nature and human destruction is not his wish,
He would be happy if all was calm and everybody would together fish.
Some will believe and others will not,
Some will go to heaven and other will in hell rot.
This poem for now has no ending,
As time goes on they will know where he will them be sending.

# Golfing Lesson

He wanted to learn how to play golf so he decided to take a lesson,
He was hoping that it would turn out to be a blessing.
He arrived early to loosen up a little,
He didn't realize he was so thick in the middle.
When the instructor arrived the lesson they did start,
Contorting his hands for the proper grip did smart.
He finally started to feel good,
So he started addressing the ball with a wood.
To swing correctly his stomach was in the way,
To change his swing might also require a hospital stay.
They worked a while longer and finally his body quit hurting,
After more hours swinging the club his hands had blood squirting.
The instructor said they should stop the lesson for today,
For he was not improving very fast anyway.

# Good Programmer vs Poor Programmer

Some computer programmers are highly skilled,
When you find one, they are strong willed.
They are very efficient in what they do,
The poor programmers don't have a clue.
The skilled programmer spends 95% of their time thinking,
The poor programmer spends 55% of their time thinking and drinking.
The skilled programmer spends 3% of their time writing code,
The poor programmer spends 20% of their time writing code when in the mode.
The skilled programmer spends 2% of their time doing 3 compiles with a perfect result,
The poor programmer spends 25% of their time running compiles that are an insult.
I know this because Dennis Mendon, a friend of mine who has past was very good,
He amazed me with his ability for 1 or 2 compiles and the program on its own stood.

# Grandma's Apple Pie

When I was small our trips to grandma's house were fun,
All the wide open spaces where we could run.
The best part of going to grandma's farm was her apple pie,
It smelled and looked so good it was a pleasure to the eye.
When grandma hollered the pie is ready,
We all ran to the house so fast we had a hard time standing steady.
As she put the ice cream on the pie you could almost feel it melt,
Everybody's mouth watered and really good felt.
As the hot pie and ice cream touches your fork,
You also remember that for supper you had delicious pork.
When the hot pie countered by the cold ice cream passes you taste buds,
You keep it in your mouth longer by chewing it as a cow chews its cud.
We want to go to grandmas all the time,
Because after eating pie she reads us rhymes.
Grandmas gone now but when times are bad we think of grandma's apple pie,
I can tell you friend; that is no lie.

# Graveyard Shift

Graveyard people are a special kind,
Too stay awake they have to be creative with their minds.
Tick, tock, tick, tock, the minutes slip by,
Some shifts they look in the mirror and ask why.
They learn a new dance to keep the blood moving,
Some of them really start to get grooving.
The newspapers give them a break at four,
They draw names to see who gets this chore.
Their duty is to let the residents sleep sound,
They keep an eye open for any scoundrels hanging around.
They are the first officers residents see at the break of a new day,
Which sets the residents tone in a happy way.
Don't worry graveyard, you are doing fine,
Close to morning you can look for Day Shifts sign.

# Grieving Process

Everybody grieves in their own way,
Death affects people different every day.
The initial shock of death hits everybody hard,
Some deaths seem like they have always been in the cards.
When death is instantaneous for someone,
The survivors feel like they have been hit by a bullet from a gun.
When death is long and drawn out for some,
The initial impact hits just as hard when it comes.
Church bereavement groups can help people through it,
People need to find out they are not alone when they lonely get.
Some people grieve for what is a short time,
Others end up grieving for a long period which is an anguishing kind.
When a loved one or a friend is taken we ask why,
We will never know, but in Gods master plan it was their time to die.
The best way to ease the grief of losing a loved one or a friend some day,
Is to build a strong support structure and use it in any way.

# Hands from God

Her hands were sent from God,
It was very special what she could do with a metal rod.
Her sculptures can be seen around the world,
People stand in "ah" looking at the way the rods are curled.
Her talent working with metal rods was self taught,
She learned to do this when she decided it was something she sought.
The feel of the metal in her hands is like putty,
This is a skill that came naturally; she did not have to study.
Her surname was Keller so they gave her Helen for her first name,
After another blind lady who rose to the top of her game.

# Happy

This poem is about being happy,
Happy people smile and are snappy.
Happy people walk briskly and hold their head high,
It makes other people raise up and wonder why.
You can see a special hitch in their get up and go,
Happy can be contagious and a happy person will tell you so.
A happy person smiles in the morning clear through to the night,
If you ask them why they always smile, they will say "That's right".
When they walk into any room their brightness takes over,
When they walk by the neighbor's dog, it even brightens rover.
As Forest might say "Happy is what happy does", with a happy face,
Stay happy and make the world a happier place.

# Harold and Ethel Hall's 50th Wedding Anniversary

Nineteen Forty-Eight was the beginning of it all,
Two people in love whose names are Harold and Ethel Hall,
Yerington, Nevada was where they called home,
Such a pretty place, they had no need to roam,
Through the years they raised four children in their haven,
Beautiful daughters Linda, Sandy, Debbie and handsome son David,
Their parenting skills proved to be the best,
For all their children turned out a little better than the rest,
Fifty years later you wonder where the time has gone,
But then you start looking at the next fifty that are just over the dawn,
This poem brings with it many more happy wishes,
Which will come true if Harold ever does the dishes.

Both Harold and Ethel have passed away. I included this poem as a tribute to their lives.

# Hastie's Pest Control, Las Vegas, Nevada

Have you ever had that feeling on your arm,
Of something crawling on you feeling warm.
Have you ever opened a cupboard door,
To find creepy crawlers moving around to your horror.
Call Mark Hastie because he's the man,
Hastie's Pest Control will be there in a hurry with an exact plan.
There is no safe place for insects to hide in this land,
If Hastie Pest Control can't destroy them nobody can.
The insects run and try to hide anywhere,
But wherever they go Hastie's Pest Control will quickly be there.
If you want to sleep as snug as a kitten,
Call Hastie's Pest Control before you are bitten.

# HATRED

Hatred is usually created through fear,
Many who have racial hatred need to look in a mirror.
Some people have had physical confrontations that make them that way,
They can see the physical scares and cannot change their mind to this day.
If they really stopped and thought a while,
It is not the color of the attacker's skin that makes them stink like a pile.
It doesn't matter if his attackers were white, black, brown or yellow,
His attackers could have been any of these; it is their soul that is not mellow.
If people of one race are outnumbered by people of another race fear comes into play.
Everybody's fear comes from the unknown of the next moment of their everyday,
This unknown makes some people cry and others pray.
These fears are not new; they were there as baby Jesus lay in a manger of hay.
It is sad to say that hatred of all kinds will never go away,
Hatred was built into our psychological makeup during our birth and is here to stay.
Since hatred is here to stay,
Harmony is the word we need to preach day by day.
If we can all learn to live together and control hatred at a low level,
Harmony will over shadow hatred and straightened out the squire's bevel.
This poem is not about stopping hatred in the world; there is no way,
Hopefully whoever reads this will share it to get people thinking more every day.

# He Knew it was the End

The blood oozed from the hole in his chest,
He knew it would not be long before he was looking at his final rest.
He felt that sense that he was not long for this life,
He was sorry that he would not be able to say goodbye to his children and his wife.
He knew that it was wrong for him the bank rob,
He blocked it out of his mind and treated it like a job.
He thought he would be safe if he got to his car,
But the police were behind him and he had not gone far.
The gun he had was old,
But in his hand it made him feel bold.
In a panic he knew he could not face his family now,
He figured he would end up dead but he did not know how.
He turned to look at the police and the gun slipped from his hand,
The gun hit the floor and exploded, the bullet into his body did land.
His panic made him numb to the pain,
Outside the car it has just started to rain.
For the family, he did not want to die,
But for what he did he knew for a long time in prison he would lie.
He knew the police would be wondering about the shot,
He knew he had to give up because the pain hurt a lot.
He knew he had just cost his family a lot of grief,
In a few moments he had changed his mind and hoped death would be brief.
He died there alone in his car that day,
Leaving his family to wonder if there had been another way.

# He Tried

He was elected and thrilled to be going to Washington D.C. soon,
He was anxious to implement his campaign promises made under the moon.
His first days in Washington were a thrill,
Then he was told he had to read 300 bills.
He had to fight to get his bills into play,
When he got to talk he landed on deaf ears what he had to say.
He kept trying while hitting his head against the political wall,
Everybody said he was trouble because he would not play ball.
The good ole boys knew all the illegal tricks,
They appeared to use bribery and extortion to get their special projects into the mix.
He was reelected for a second term,
None of his bills were confirmed.
After two terms he left a defeated broken man,
It is alleged that the U.S. Congress is the most corrupt group in the land.
Many years later these were his last words before he died,
"Please forgive me people for I tried".

# Healthy; Not

They say the air you breathe can kill,
These days everybody should have a will.
Diet soda will turn you into a chemical puddle one day,
Why worry about it when you can also die a million other ways.
Safe sex is getting harder to define,
Especially when you have had too much wine.
Eating oysters in a month without a R,
Is supposed to keep you away from an Oyster Bar.
They say that flying will put you underground,
Who cares for eventually you will be under a mound.
If you do not do what they say that can cause you harm,
You will not leave the bunker waiting for the nuclear alarm.

# His Big Race

Boy, I feel good today,
I want to get my short workout over early no matter what they say.
Six hours to the race,
All I need to do is keep up a good pace.
It is time for me to get a good rub down,
I love to listen to that soothing musical sound.
It is time to get dressed,
While having my legs taped and the saddle tightened I start to get stressed.
It is time for my warm up,
The dog that keeps me calm is just a pup.
Here we go out to the track,
I wonder if they bet on me a big money stack.
As we move to the gate,
Many others have an increased heart rate.
The bell rang and the gates opened at last,
All of us bolted out of the gates really fast.
This race is one mile long.
I need to pace myself so I can stay strong.
I'm in fifth place at the half,
I'm felling so good I would like to laugh.
At the three quarter mark I have moved to second place,
I'm starting to get winded at this pace.

I jerk my head to get more rein,
I want to win this race no matter the pain.
As three of us passed the finish line,
It was too close to know if the race was mine.
The twenty minutes it took to say who won,
It was for all of us no fun.
When it was announced that I had won by three inches at the finish,
Even though it was only three inches the win it did not diminish.
This was my first win and it was very special to me,
I was not supposed to live at birth you see.
It was a hard birth for my mother that night,
She died while I was being born which was not a pretty sight.
I was hand fed for weeks,
Because I was very meek.
By winning this race,
It helped many people save face.

# His First Birthday (Babies View)

Oh no; not a bath in the morning,
Especially without a warning.
What is so special about today,
I do not feel different in any way.
There are many people here, I do not know,
I'm scared of most of them; I might pottie go.
What is this bright paper they want me to grab and tear,
When I did this yesterday, mom slapped my hand but with care.
OK; I did it with your help mom,
What is it; I see the name on the side is Tom.
There, the paper is off the box,
Hey, that baby girl over there is a fox.
These things make noise and are fun to spin,
There is so much stuff here; this is really a win.
I'm hungry when are we going to eat,
There are two cakes, eating both of them will be a feat.
Why do I get the small one first,
After eating this I will have a strong thirst.
This is sure fun covering my hands, face and belly with cake,
My mom is not even trying to me clean make.
Hey, where did everybody go,
I have not begun to put on my spoiled show.
Two baths in one day,
I'm tired and need to hit the hay.

# Holocaust

Holocaust is a word that brings back nightmares and mental scares to many still alive,
There was terror in some nationalities in Europe that at Dachau they would arrive.
I have a problem with people that continue to say the Holocaust did not exist,
My wife and I walked through Dachau and the sorrow in our heart we could not resist.
We stood where the people's housing was located in the camp,
The chill you felt could on your heart leave a permanent stamp.
We walked slowly through the actual showers that spewed deadly gas,
Let the people that do not believe its existence; walk now this path.
After the showers, we passed and looked into the horrifying furnaces they used,
Close your eyes and you could almost feel the heat and see the frail bodies without shoes.
Around the world today this same type of travesty has played out more than it should.
Anything like this is a horrible situation for all; when will it everywhere stop for good.

# How Many Cowboy Boots Are Enough

Can you have too many cowboy boots?,
My answer is "NO" as I buy another pair just for a hoot.
There are cowboy boots for riding, walking, rodeo, work and bowling to name a few,
My wife on the other hand believes having all those cowboy boots means I lost a screw.
There are work cowboy boots for mud, dirt, sand, scaffolds and just fun,
My wife feels that when I reached 16 pair, I had spent too much time in the sun.
Cowboy boots are very comfortable to wear,
Some have such a design that people stare.
Most are worn under your pant leg every day,
Some are worn with your pant legs inside the cowboy boots; also a normal way.
I saved one pair of cowboy boots from the dump,
I converted them to bowling cowboy boots; I did not fall on my rump.
Cowboy boots are just like anything else you cherish,
You will do anything to ensure that they do not perish.

# I Am Me

The first 14 years of my life I felt were normal,
My parents were well known and everything was always formal.
In my 15th year I could feel a change that at first scared me,
My body was changing, but my mind was telling me I needed to decide who to be.
When I was with my friends, we talked about the opposite sex almost every day,
I listened but my body was not responding as the others would say.
As time went on I started to notice things about members of my own gender the most,
This made me feel different, but if I told my parents I would be toast.
Mentally it was causing me to feel ill all the time holding it in,
It did not help when in church they called it a sin.
When in college I met another student who felt the same as I did,
We decided to experiment but keep our actions under a lid.
One day we decided we did not want to hide it anymore,
My friend's parents already knew and mine surprised me by not hitting the floor.
I felt born again within myself,
From that day on I have had perfect health.
I am happy as can be now that I know who I was born to be,
My partner and I give thanks everyday that we live in the land of the free.

# Improving Her Self Esteem

Every morning she surveyed herself in the mirror,
What she saw did not make her cheer.
Her hair, face and most parts of her body are fine,
Her breasts had always been small and a reason for her to pine.
She works with other women, who have increased their breasts,
They seemed so much more confident than the rest.
She made an appointment for the procedure in one week,
She decided her boyfriend would be the first to peek.
To improve her self confidence she was hell bent,
The day of the procedure came and went.
She looked in the mirror and saw two perfect mounds,
Her body was fine and it looked like she had lost pounds.
Her boyfriend did a somersault with glee,
I know they are for you but Thank You from me.
Her mother told her she looked fine,
Then added "I wish they were mine.".
When she returned to work everybody said she looked good,
Many female friends were impressed and wish they also could.
Her self esteem was immediately raised,
Men have to watch how their words are phrased.
She is no longer blue,
But now she cannot see her shoes.

# Indian's Point of View

We have lived on this land for hundreds of years,
To keep it we have shed thousands of tears.
We can roam farther than a 60 day ride,
Be it winter, spring, summer or fall, we keep our stride.
We move with Tatonka for its hide, meat and bones; when they arrive.
These things clothed, fed and helped us survive.
We fought with other tribes for coup and horses; not land,
We stayed away from the desert where other tribes learned to live in the sand.
Then came the white man who wanted our land and change our life,
They came with their belongings, children and their wife.
They signed treaties with us,
Then broke them right away which made us cuss.
They killed Tatonka for only the tongue and hides,
This waste of good meat and bones made it hard for us to be on their side.
Then we were fighting to keep our land and be free,
They even built houses with many of the trees.
Our fighting ability was better than theirs,
They finally won because of their larger numbers and many heirs.
They forced us onto small pieces of land,
Where we did not have enough people to put up a stand.
Here we are now having to watch for them to bring meals of meat,
Most of the meat was no good from setting too long in the heat.
All our great warriors are now gone from this earth,
But we still believe in the value of our worth.
Reservations killed our way of life,
For our warriors, their children and wife.

# Inspection Time

We were going along fine,
Then the news came that hit us like a mine.
At the beginning of our shift plus two hours,
The inspector will be here and he is not bringing flowers.
Pressed suit, ironed shirt, polished shoes and all the rest,
Where is my shoe polish I need to pass this test.
There is always pressure to look real good,
Aren't we always supposed to look as good as we could.
Here comes the inspector, he sure looks mad,
After all my work, if he tears me up I will be sad.
He starts with my hair but stops at my nose,
Hopefully my breath smells like a rose.
He checks my mustache, especially the corners of my lip,
If it extends beyond the corners he will flip.
He checks my tie to see if it is straight,
The alignment of my suit coat and trousers must also be first rate.
I am glad that I wore black socks tonight,
If anything; at least I got that right.
When he got to my shoes I saw him scrunch his brow,
I was waiting for him to have a cow.
Then he gave me a sly smile as to say,
You pass the inspection in all ways.
As he walked away I could see a rip in his trousers and laughed for a while,
When he noticed it, he gave me a shy smile.
I passed the inspection with flying colors today,
I was perfect in any and all ways.

# Invisible Moose

My wife and I have always wanted to see a real moose,
A real one out where they run loose.
In Montana we were told that you can see one every day by the lake,
For many days we drove by the lake but not one Moose did we pictures take.
Our next try was a cruise to Alaska in May,
And do you think we would see a Moose; not even through the last day.
We are currently back in the land of palm trees and sun,
We can continue to look at the Moose pictures on the wall and envision how they run.
We know that someday our dream will come true,
But until then I guess we will sit in Las Vegas and be blue.

# Janet's Fear

Janet's is the receptionist for Mr. Johnson without a day off,
She books his appointments and ensures all the women find their way to his loft.
He doesn't try to hide anything from her,
Even the sexual escapades after the women were to the loft lured.
She does not agree with what goes on in the loft at night,
She knows in her heart that those things are not right.
She knows that his wife sits in the mansion all alone,
Waiting to hear from him on the phone.
He thinks he is pretty smart and nobody knows about the loft,
He is not very quiet about it so his head must be soft.
A couple of nights ago while he slept, four slugs made him permanently sleep,
During his funeral, nobody including his wife did weep.
His first name was Lenny,
His wife told the judge, he had played her for a fool on time to many.
After hearing her story and seeing all the bruises, the judge gave her three years,
Janet's fear was losing her job, but still; Mr. Johnson's death did not bring any tears.
Janet is still working there for a new boss,
She agrees that losing Mr. Johnson was not a big loss.

# Joey

Joey seemed a little slow to most,
But that was not the feeling of his host.
He was born of a mother on weed,
But she never did heed.
She would leave his alone for days,
For no one to take care of him in any way.
His cries could be heard all night,
When the police arrived he was in a fright.
Thirsty, hungry and soiled he survived this living hell,
It was amazing that he became well.
With the first six months of his life behind him now,
Every chance he got he would eat more chow.
His physical stature grew strong and fast,
But his mental state put him in his class last.
The other children teased him all the time,
His favorite drink is cherry-lime.
Over the years Joey learned how to adjust,
He worked harder because he knew he must.
Joey was not as slow as most people thought,
He refused to lay back and let his brain rot.
With all of his new parents desire and love,
He decided to study birds of which one was a dove.
Joey went on to a successful life,
He lived many years with his beautiful wife.

# John Hambrick for Assembly

John Hambrick is his name,
Providing outstanding support to his constituents is his game.
As a Nevada State Assemblyman from District 2,
None of his constituents will ever need to be blue.
With his background in Law Enforcement he has the skill,
To work with people and not create a chill.
His dedication to adults and children together,
Gives him the strength to survive the political weather.
His volunteerism is dear to his heart,
To see the Little League kid's smiles is like beautiful art.
His reelection bid for the Nevada State Assembly is going strong,
When you vote for John Hambrick you will never be wrong.

# Key and Lock

There is a special key that fits a very special lock,
This lock cannot be broken with a rock.
This lock protects one man's most valuable possession,
This lock is not affected by recession.
This lock is not necessarily a woman's best friend,
This lock can make it hard for her to bend.
When the key is slid into the lock each time,
If it will not unlock, the man will whine.
But when the key does open the lock it is a happy day,
The man and woman celebrate this opportunity in many ways.
The year was 1886 and the location was France,
The chastity belt fit perfect over her underpants.

# Killing Morale

The people worked hard to do the job right,
The company policy on write ups was tight.
The supervisors were given quotas for their shift,
This micromanagement does nothing more than to cause a rift.
People are too nervous to do their job correct,
This type of micromanagement does not help people to connect.
People will not stay when the purpose of the company is to find them wrong,
They will find out people will not stay because they are strong.
If a company has to use these scare tactics to feel good,
Then they need robots and not human beings that they want to act like wood.

# Laid Off

I went to work that day feeling spry and fine,
Not knowing that I would leave feeling like I had been dropped in a mine.
I was told I was laid-off that day,
I sure didn't feel like I lived in the land of milk and honey in any way.
I went home and told my wife,
We knew this was going to change our life.
We had to trade in a big vehicle for a smaller car,
We did not; but some people would have headed straight for the bar.
We cut back to try and save some money,
My wife took it all in stride, she is my special honey.
I started sending out resumes left and right,
All the rejection letters made me want to fight.
It is now one year and over a thousand resumes later,
The interviews and no job could make a person a hater.
We have been able to survive till now,
But from here on out we are not sure how.
To miss our first payment ever is hard to take,
Next month is the first month we will not this make.
The government says there are many programs for us,
The red tape for these programs can make a preacher cuss.
In the end we decided to walk away,
We will live with it until we are dead and gray.

# Las Vegas, Nevada Youth

There is a segment of the Las Vegas youth, who will never be normal in any way,
They have never had to live in the real world on any day.
I call them the blind rich in this city,
All they see is money and they think that they are witty.
From Disneyland trips four times a year from two years old,
To a new Porsche every year of High School, all they know is cash that is cold.
Their parents have taught them that they are above the law,
For they believe that any deal for them would never be raw.
They have never known what it is to be poor,
They have never had to start anything up from the floor.
Every time that they do something wrong,
Their parent's lawyer comes on strong.
Las Vegas is a town built on image and money,
Parents will spend millions to keep their image at times and that aint funny.
Once in a great while the rich will spend time in jail,
They will still have the butler deliver their mail.
The only things they learn in High School is who they can buy and what will it cost,
Their sense of honesty and compassion is forever lost.
It is sad each day when we have to say,
For a segment of youth in Las Vegas, this is the normal way.

# Last Day

This is my last day here,
Sometimes you are sad and other times you cheer.
If you like the job,
You can never be a slob.
If you hate the job,
It is easy to be a snob.
Either way those last moments seem to be strange,
All the knowledge you gained will expand your range.
As with your personal life, at work you leave friends behind,
Some you will stay in contact with and others you will never again find.
Security is like a law enforcement position in some ways,
Hours of calm broken by minutes of chaos every day.
Some things you will always miss,
While others when you remember will make you hiss.
Three hours to go until it is the end,
Then when the move is over you will with new people blend.
My shift is over and it s time to go,
Goodbye everybody and keep up a smiling glow.

## Life's Lesson

She raised her shirt to show two perfect beauties,
It was a dare from her friends who are cuties.
She laughed as they showed her the shot,
She had no idea how much trouble she had caught.
Two weeks later her boss called her in to talk,
He showed her the picture and said she would have to walk.
He said the picture was online and stated the Companies name,
Two sponsors cancelled because they didn't want the same.
The lesson here is that your actions can cost you,
You have to think twice about what you do.

# Life's Trials

Most people want to have a quiet solid life,
They normally intend to stay away from strife.
This is a good feeling while it lasts,
But these things can change really fast.
Changes in personnel at the top,
Can make everything good stop.
When life takes a 180 degree turn it forces you to adjust,
You can get mad and fight it but in the end change you must.
There is a lot of good in the world but a few who are evil can cause a lot more stress,
You cannot let the evil take control, you must evil head on address.
When evil causes many problems they think they are bright,
Unfortunately for the evil people they will never see the light.
To beat them you can never let them win,
Their day of reckoning will come when the Lord counts their sins.

# Lost Calf

It was June 24th, 1968; the 16th year of my birth to the day,
I was visiting my great uncle's farm which I loved in a special way.
I had thoughts of visiting my friends in town,
Then my great uncle shot those plans down.
He said that a mother cow had come home alone,
Her new born calf was somewhere in the pasture possibly scared to the bone.
We saddled up Flicka and Pontiac to head to the pasture by the path,
We left the mother cow in the barn as to not receive her wrath.
We spent hours in the saddle looking for a place the newborn calf could hide,
By evening we really wanted to have the calf by its mother's side.
At the far end of the pasture the calf appeared; lying in a large bush snug as a bug.
We were glad when evening fell and the calf was by his mother laying in hay soft as a rug.
Yes, I missed seeing my friends on that special day,
But I would never have given up this experience in any way.

# Lost Pay Check

I get paid every week,
A little enjoyment I do seek.
I usually limit myself to twenty bucks,
Then I wish for a lot of luck.
The slot machine is my nemesis for this game,
I know that playing these slots will never bring me fame.
I remember one night a while back,
I drank too much and good senses I did lack.
A beautiful young lady sat beside me and wished me the best,
After more than my quantity to drink, it is hard to tell the rest.
I remember spending a lot of money as she whispered in my ear,
After way too much to drink, I overcame any fear.
I woke up the next morning in my rented room,
When I opened my eyes and moved my head, everything went boom.
I finally made it to the shower and breakfast ate,
It is good it is the weekend or I would be for work late.
When I collected my money from all my pockets,
I wished I was going for a ride away on a rocket.
When I counted all my money,
I wanted to cry because it was not funny.
I had spent one whole weeks check in one night,
Then I realized I have not paid my rent, I was in quite a fright.

# Love from Afar

I first saw her from across the room,
My eyes started blinking from the dust created by the broom.
I looked again and her hair was like silk and down her back,
My mind started wondering about the size of her rack.
Her arms seemed a little large but also soft,
My mind wondered again if I could get her to my loft.
I walked to her and her legs were a little heavy; she wore heels of white,
The closer I got she wore a big diamond ring that was bright.
I slid in beside her and asked if I could buy her a drink,
I envisioned her face all rosy pink.
She said "Yes" and turned to face me,
With that dark beard I realized that she was a he.
The look on my face could have stopped a clock,
My heart felt like a big wooden block.
I excused myself from the table,
I drank three shots as quick as I was able.
I don't have an opinion about people that cross dress,
It is not for me, even though I think of them no less.

# Lying Wannabees

When you work security at a high end condo at night,
Many of the visitors will never tell you right.
If you ask them a question they will say yes,
When they know that their reply is not yes, but a lot less.
These people that lie to security are visiting rich friends that day,
They think they are better because of their rich friends, but no way.
They are actually showing their true color and lack of morals to all,
It would be nice to be there when they fall.

# Maiden 1, Vampire 0

Her clothes were ripped as she ran through the trees,
She would run a ways; then she would freeze.
She could feel he was out there,
No matter how hard she looked, she did not know where.
She could not see him flying above,
Measuring her up like a tight fitting glove.
The further she ran the more skin he saw,
From high above he could not see a flaw.
The sight of her blood gave him a chill,
To stop from draining her dry, he had not the will.
He swooped down and changed from bat to man,
To drain her quickly was his plan.
He knew she would fall under his spell,
He knew that with her blood he would feel well.
As he covered her with his cape,
She knew this was her last chance to escape.
She could feel his breath on her neck so bare,
She thrust the stack into his heart through his chest hair.
His demise was quite a sight,
She walked out of the woods at first light.

# Main Gates

Here we go again the other half of the gate and I,
The way they keep coming in I think I need a shot of rye.
We no sooner close and another car drives up,
The way we go back and forth we need more oil than a cup.
Be it 115 degrees or 30 degrees we faithfully perform our duties,
But we feel lucky because we get to see all the cuties.
Back and forth we all day long go,
We work as requested; hard as can be but never for a show.
As long as we have oil and power we will never drain,
Our elbows take the most strain.
Every once in a while a part of us gets tired,
But we know we are needed and will never be fired.
We know we will be here long after many residents are gone,
We are the proud entrance gates of Golden Lawn.

# Mandy's First Snow

Living in south Texas there is no snow,
It has been this way for 70 years in a row.
We decided to take Mandy with us up north,
So we packed the car and Mandy and set forth.
We made it to Minnesota without much trouble,
The only thing we had was a tire with a bubble.
On the second day there the snow came fast,
Luckily it did not for very long last.
Mandy ran off the deck onto the snow and was no longer there,
She yelped and jumped on the deck from what seemed like nowhere.
She shook off the snow and looked up at me and growled,
Then on her face she gave me a scrawl.
She then looked at her indention in the snow so deep,
She starred at it trying to figure out how she ended up in a heap.
She touched the snow gingerly with her paw,
The cold feeling made her paw burn like it was raw.
She ran to the door and whined to get out of the cold,
At that moment she did not seem like she was bold.
Each time she went out she traveled less,
So I ended up picking up her mess.
By the time we left for home one day,
Mandy was familiar with the snow in many ways.

# Mark the Brave

Mark was working on dissolving a bee hive one day,
He had done this many times his special way.
He mixed the chemicals and waited for the best time to spray,
When he started to spray; he was sure the bees would have something to say.
Mark is allergic to bee stings so he takes special care,
He looks like something from a Mel Brooks movie with the outfit he wears.
He thought the spray had killed all the bees,
He removed most of the hive when he had to freeze.
Two very large bees were staring him right in the eye,
They turned to show him their strong and long stingers and he wondered why.
They flew away and then he felt a bump on his rump.
They had flown off to a very high stump.
He said "Oh no, I have to go",
As he ran through the weeds in his suit, it was quite a show.
He looked like Buck Rogers trying to fly,
If he could he would have headed for the sky.
As he got in his truck he gave a sigh of relief,
Then he stared at the window in disbelief.
The two bees were staring at him, seeming to say "Com out and play",
As Mark drove away, he laughed as he said "Maybe another day".

# Marriage

Marriage is the legal means to be together,
She thought she knew him until he brought out the leather.
She gave a big sigh of relief,
When he told her the leather was for his belief.
It has always been his good luck charm,
Since he has owned it he has had no harm.
There are many words that make up the love between a husband and wife,
Some are minor but this one must be there for life.
The word that means the most is TRUST,
This word keeps the marriage strong so it will not rust.
You can have trust without love, but it helps.
You cannot have true love without trust which makes it hard on the little whelps.
As the marriage goes on little things might pile up,
But trust will keep you from running over your cup.
As you celebrate your 50th Anniversary that all long-term marriages must,
You will agree one of the major reasons you are celebrating your 50th is trust.

# Military Spouses

Military spouses are the best,
They have to be better than the rest.
Their partner can be gone for long periods of time,
Protecting our freedom while fighting in the mud and slime.
At home the spouse holds down the fort,
They could also hold down the base or the port.
The spouse must do it all,
Be it summer, spring, winter or fall.
The children, the car, school and the dog,
It is enough to put you in a permanent fog.
There are many civilian spouses that have the same issues,
But their partners are not in a position that daily could require tissues.
Their partners are protecting the freedom of US citizens many places around this earth,
Their partners training will ensure that their partner will fight for all their worth.
The military spouse is the backbone of each marriage,
Their support allows their partner to fight without worrying about the baby carriage.
The poem is for the spouses of all fighting men and women in the five services today,
Their partners have made it possible for us to live the American Way.
Army, Navy, Air Force, Marines and Coast Guard for one and all,
They are all together when they get the call.

# Moms

Moms cry when you are born,
Moms cry when you are scorned.
Moms cry when you are hurt,
Moms cry when you have a girlfriend and flirt.
Moms cry when you go to the prom,
Moms cry when their son's new boyfriend is named Tom.
Moms cry when you graduate from school,
Moms cry when you break a golden rule.
Moms cry when you give them their first grandchild,
Moms cry when you are sick though mild.
Moms cry to show their love,
Moms cry when they pray to the Lord above.
Do not get this poem wrong,
Moms are very strong.
Moms cry about all these things,
Because with the tears, exceptional love clings.

# Money Does Not Buy Respect

In this land of milk and honey,
There are many people with a lot of money.
Those that earned it are more subdued by it,
Those that inherit it seem to flaunt it which does not fit.
Respect must be earned, not given by rights,
Those that think money gives them respect have lost sight.
Power can give people a false sense of respect the same as money,
For everybody who has to be around them; life is not funny.
People who become instantly rich feel it gives them many things it does not,
When their old and new friends start waning, they are left to rot.
When respect has been earned, hard work and common sense are the reason,
Those that think it should be automatically given to them are out of season.
As the title says "Money Does Not Buy Respect" and this is a true line,
Those that think different are bound for unhappy times.

# Moving Blues

Life is not always fair,
Sometimes a group of friends lose a pair.
When they have to move away,
It is sometimes hard on the ones who have to stay.
A voice on the phone is never the same as a face,
The words though can warm a soul and move a person to another place.
The memories are many and long,
As special as the memories are, remembering them will never steer you wrong.
As you get older, losing face to face contact gets harder for all,
Ones heart starts to ache waiting for the other one to call.
Time heals some of the heartache,
These types of friendships, distance cannot break.
I always say that the only thing static in life is change,
This is a fact whether it is sunshine or rain.
People are always stronger in these situations than what they give themselves for credit,
Sometimes though when you have to succumb to the blues, let it.
You might think that everything will never be the same,
You can search your soul but cannot locate who is to blame.
This person or that might seem to have gotten the ball rolling,
But other factors have to come into play to keep everything flowing.
Some friends who have moved a lot, making and losing friends might be easier for them.
It is; when you are younger, but age adds more emotion to the process when.
Distance can not diminish true friend's feelings,
It also cannot stop a broken heart from healing.
Times like this are usually reflected as sorrow by most of us,
It should be a time of joy; your friends are moving on to something better and not fuss.
Hold your chin up and give a smile,
Let your friends remember this last look from across the miles.

# Moving Home

Forty years ago I moved away from home to be married,
Now I am moving back home and in the future to be buried.
My life as an Army wife took me too many places,
I lived a good life and made friend from many races.
The last four times we moved; each move was suppose to be the last,
Then the trials and tribulations of life stepped in and again; reflections of the past.
As you pack box after box after box throughout each day,
You come across stuff you have not used in years, but decide to keep it anyway.
As the last box is loaded on the moving truck,
You hope that the condition of everything at the other end does not suck.
Home is where I want to now be,
I want to get there; settle down and stay low key.
The house I grew up in might be the one for me,
Only time will tell so we will have to wait and see.
It will be good to visit with old friends and family again,
Some of them I have not seen since I do not remember when.
At 58 and 53, each move is physically harder on us,
No matter how slow we take it, it is quite a fuss.
Most of our items will end up in storage,
With the cost of this move we will probably end up eating porridge.
Moving to the upper Midwest during the month of November,
Hopefully it does not turn into a trip from hell to remember.
This poem is finished for now,
When the move is over I will then tell you how.

## Mrs. Bach's Class

Mrs. Bach's class is the best,
Always a notch higher than the rest.
Their poem and names helped our pain,
It turned our day into sunshine, instead of rain.
Our cat was given Sadie for a name,
Bringing joy and happiness to our life was her game.
She was 19 when she got to the meadow by the ridge,
To wait for us with her sisters and brothers, until we cross heavens bridge.
Waldi, Gypsy, Boots, Riley, Nikki, Brittnee, Gyver, Merlin and Rascal cry tears,
All the pets that have graced our life over the last 34 wonderful years.
Sadie will be in good company with all of them until we are there,
When Sandy and I are together with all of them as the last pair.

# My Bear

I was riding on the high range on day,
The grass was not tall but I decided to move the horses anyway.
I was heading home when my horse spooked and I hit the ground,
I was stunned but forced myself to look around.
I saw the bear that spooked my horse and it was coming on night,
I knew to come out of this I was going to have to fight.
My horse was long gone with my Winchester tied to the saddle,
I looked for something to scare the bear that would rattle.
Before I could move the bear was beside me,
He sniffed my hair and then I knew I could not run free.
I felt his claws draw blood on my back,
I tried to play dead and as limp as a burlap sack.
As he ripped my clothes and skin to try and expose my face,
My blood ran freely and I felt like I was in deaths place.
As I started to pass out I heard a big boom,
I felt more pain as the bear broke my leg for there was no other room.
When my horse returned, the ranch foreman came looking for me,
He shot the bear just as he was about to make me no longer to be.
I recovered from my injuries except for a slight limp on my left leg,
The bears head hangs in the ranch house from a very large peg.
On the cold nights I am very warm as I go to sleep,
I cover myself with the bear's hide as I lay beneath it in a heap.

# My Cousins 409

My cousin had a Chevy with a 409,
It was cool to listen to that motor whine.
The three deuces on top of the motor took space,
When the motor was fired up you knew it was intended to race.
The four speed on the floor,
When in first really made that motor roar.
As he hit second gear boy did those tires squeal,
The power of that motor made you hold on tight to the steering wheel.
When he slapped third gear boy it started to fly,
As the telephone poles went by like fence posts you did not have to ask why.
Fourth gear comes about in a flash,
The adrenaline that passed through your body was a blast.
As the speed touched 140 MPH it was time to bring it down,
Actually 140 MPH was to fast as the red light behind us went round and round.

# My First Car

Saturday, the day that took three weeks in one week to get there,
I was up early waiting for my father who came from I know not where.
I had never known him to move so slow,
All I wanted was to get in the car and roll.
With my saved money we were buying my first car today,
I knew what I wanted but only had so much to down lay.
I saw my car on the lot,
But when we checked it had already been bought.
It wasn't my car to be,
So we drove farther to look at whatever we could see.
We looked most of the day and decided to head for home,
I figured that for another week I would be walking alone.
Then my father said "What is that back in the corner?" with four doors,
I could see my friends not wanting to ride in it; what a bore.
Within a week I was driving to school,
I drove real slow as I went by the girls at the pool.
I drove my girlfriend out by the stream,
Driving my girlfriend around in my own car felt like a dream.

# My Friend Bert Fitch

A friend like Bert Fitch is hard to find,
In fact another does not come to mind.
In the computer room our minds worked as one,
We accomplished all the work and made it fun.
The Army and life kept us apart,
But nothing could change the feelings in our hearts.
Cancer and other medical issues keep kicking him in the ass,
But no matter what happens he sees the world as a full glass.
The pain might be his alone,
But the love for him by others is readily shown.
This test; that needle they never seem to end,
Please Lord do not let any of those needles bend.
His enthusiasm for life makes everybody's day bright,
You don't have to know him long to know he is right.
Though he is old; well older than me,
He is always as young as he wants to be.
Keep going dear friend don't let it get you down,
We want you with us for many more years around.

# My Friend from Town

I grew up poor on a mountain side,
To get to school was a long horse ride.
One Christmas I received my first pair of shoes,
We were poor but we lived by the rules.
In school was a boy from town,
He had new clothes, but his face was always in a frown.
One day I asked him why,
I also asked him not to lie.
He asked me why I always had a smile,
When I had no shoes and rode a horse for miles.
He said his mom loved him so,
While his step-dad did not care if he would go.
I asked if he wanted to come home with me,
He said he would ask his mother and see.
The next holiday he rode home behind me on my trusty steed,
With our shoes off our feet were tickled by the tall weeds.
Over the holiday he saw where my smile came from,
We listened to my father as he did the banjo strum.
Yes, we were very poor in money,
The love in our family made us very rich, like fresh milk and honey.
The next time I saw my friend from the city,
He was all smiles and giddy.
He said that his mother loved his smile so,
She told his step-dad that he had to go.

## My German Wine Fest Experience

The week before the wine fest was fun,
We worked late into the night to get everything done.
We had to make sure that the wine would last,
With the people working it could disappear fast.
Finally everything was ready for the fest,
Everybody was exhausted and deserved a rest.
When the fest started, the wine began flowing,
Soon many noses and cheeks began glowing.
The music from the James Last band played loud,
To the enjoyment of everybody in the crowd.
During the fest, the size of the small village did double,
With all that everybody drank, there was no trouble.
The annual wine fest is a rite of passage for many youth,
Not just the wine but also working at the food booth.
By the time of the night that the wine fest is shutting down,
There were not many sober people still hanging around.
The morning after the little village did not show a trace,
Of the wonderful time that everybody had in that same space.
The headache that accompanied the hangover isn't so bad,
As facing your mother or spouse in the morning, who are very mad.
All the people in the village returned to the day to day grind,
With joyful thoughts of next year's wine fest on their mind.

# My Racing History

Teenagers go to the local stock car races,
You can see the glazed expressions on their faces.
I was one of those teenagers in 1969,
I wanted to drive a car around that racetrack line.
A group of us built a car in a week,
All the required parts we quickly did seek.
The car was a 1960 Chevrolet Bel Air,
When we started the car was pretty fair.
We never won a race those nights,
We had a lot of fun though by rights.
My night to drive the car came,
I was hoping it would not rain.
I was buckled in and ready to go,
The race started a little slow.
I made it around turns one and two without a hitch,
Going into turn three I went high over the bank into the ditch.
I came back onto the track by turn four,
I could hear the crowd roar.
The car died in front of the crowd,
As the other cars went by it was loud.
The gas line broke and the gas ran onto the track,
This ended of my racing career as I was pulled into the back.
The crowd was happy because they started a fire to burn the gas,
That was my racing career first to last.

# My Spouse

There is a beautiful lady named Sandy,
Who has a dog named Mandy.
She also has three cats, Milo, Dillon and Belle,
One is big, one is shy and one came from Hell.
These pets are the joy of her life,
She is also my loving wife.
The rest of the world can go by,
If you listen close I'll tell you why.
Not that close for you can still hear,
I wouldn't want to spit in your ear.
I am her husband of 34 years,
Who sometimes does not listen to what he hears.
For too many years did he extra long at work stay,
The pets were always there when she said, Hey!.
The years finally softened his Norwegian head,
As he listened to the words that she said.
His love has never waned,
Even with the way that he has behaved.
He will try very hard for the rest of his life,
To show her how special he feels to have her for his wife.

# Nancy

There is a lady named Nancy
Whose looks and style are fancy.
Her belief in God is strong,
Any belief in God is not wrong.
The last eight years of her life have been rough,
But this little Beverly Hills lady is tough.
Her husband's death was bad,
This cut her to the bone and made her feel very sad.
Her daughter's sudden turn for the worst,
Came close to making her heart burst.
Her daughter's actions cut into her soul,
But she held together in her loving mother role.
Her daughter kept bringing her bad news,
But her love for her child would not let her daughter lose.
Her place in heaven is already reserved,
Because a seat next to God is what she deserves.

# Natures Law

The bear stood silently in the middle of the stream full of water,
The father showed the bear standing there to his daughter.
As they watch they also saw the salmon swimming upstream,
The daughter tapped herself on the cheek to make sure it wasn't a dream.
As the salmon jumped it disappeared into the bear's jaw,
This was the daughter's first experience of nature's law.
This scenario is played over and over again throughout the years,
The young lady was sad for the salmon but shed no tears.
Her father explained that the salmon were swimming upstream to lay their eggs,
These eggs will turn into little salmon fish with legs.
The daughter smiled at her father and said "Legs on a fish, this I have never seen."
Yes, you are correct; there are no legs on a salmon fish because it is nature's law.

# Never Happy

The heat of the day was a menace,
It was as painful as going to the dentist.
The direct sun would beat you down,
Where is the shade when you need it around?.
Oh, Oh, there goes my shoe this next step is going to hurt,
I know I'll pay tomorrow for going without a shirt.
I'm drinking water fast and furious,
I need to keep it up so I don't get delirious.
When I was younger I could play in the sun all day,
Now when I try something like that I end up saying "No Way".
One Hundred Fifteen degrees in Las Vegas is downright hot,
Even if your used to being in the sun a lot.
The wind will not even give you a break,
Which can make your life at stake.
This poem explains some how hot the sun can be,
When it is so hot we call it a she.
One of these days I will move where it's cooler and the slow wind chimes,
Then I'll complain because I can't get enough sun all the time.

# New Born Calf

Mom it is dark in here and it is time to see the light,
I know you are not ready for the pain; but I am right.
Can't you stop eating so much hay?,
Much more and your stomachs will be in my way.
Hey what is that touching my foot,
I promise to come easy if you do not use the hook.
He tied a rope around my feet so tight,
What is that grunting, he must be pulling with all his might.
I am starting to move up the birth canal,
My mom told me the outside smells like Chanel.
What is that cool feeling on my feet,
The farmer must be pulling while sitting on his seat.
There goes my nose,
Boy this place sure does not smell like a rose.
Ouch, you are hurting my head,
I hope waiting for me is a nice soft bed.
So that is what light looks like,
I wonder if I will be able to find my cousin Mike.
Here comes my shoulder and the rest of me fast,
I have always heard that the tail comes out last.
Ouch, hey watch it that floor is hard,
I am skinny without much lard.
Quit rubbing me with that straw it tickles my side,
I know that when I get older the farmer's son will want a ride.
Look at me I am standing up,
I am hungry, I need a teat and not a cup.
Within a week I was playing with my cousins in the field,
Our mothers will an evil stare wield.
Running, jumping, feeding from my mom,
Life is a joy for calf named Tom.

# New Computer

She removed her new computer from the box with joy,
She had saved her money to buy this toy.
She turned it on for the first time,
She heard the hard disk spin and three chimes.
She pushed the power switch on the display,
Nothing showed on the screen to her dismay.
She checked the power cord and the interface cable,
She remembered the sales woman's name was Mabel.
She waited so long for this computer she wanted to cry,
She decided to give it another try.
She wondered why a new computer would not work,
The truth is anything electrical can have a quirk.
The integrated video on the motherboard was bad,
They replaced the motherboard which made her glad.
When she tried it at home that night,
Everything turned on and worked right.
She learned an important lesson that day,
Electrical items might not work when new anyway.

# No Choice

He told her you will work for me and do what I say,
If you want to live to see another day.
She left home because she thought she had it bad,
But now everyday she is sad.
If she doesn't work when he says do it,
He takes his time when he her hits.
She has been forced to pleasure so many men every day,
To make it through she blanks it out in her own way.
To keep from doing herself harm,
She thinks of home all cozy and warm.
Once she tried to run away,
That ended up in a long hospital stay.
One day the police raided his home and took him to jail,
She did not waste any time on leaving town by rail.
Her parents cried for hours when their little girl came home,
She told them that she was sorry and would for never more roam.

# No Thought

This poem is short and sweet,
It could be about my feet.
It could be about my toes,
Maybe even about my clothes.
Then again it could be about my neck,
Or that this poem does not mean a heck.
Most poems make you think,
Then there are those that really stink.
This poem can be right in front of your face,
You can decide its place.
This poem was written on a whim,
It is also out there on a limb.
I wanted it to give you some fun,
The poem is finished I need to run.

# North Dakota

North Dakota is a state all should see,
You can feel the richness in the soil while bending on your knee.
Most of the state is as flat as a tabletop,
There are hundreds of things to see if you only stop.
All the people in the towns small and large are friendly to you,
You will feel at home even though every place is new.
Coal and Oil has always been a staple to the state,
The jobs these resources bring to the area are first rate.
The badlands in the southwest corner is a treat,
You can see buffalo, prairie dogs and other animals from your car seat.
President Theodore Roosevelt loved this land dearly,
He built a ranch on this land and cherished it sincerely.
Medora is the closest town where you can see the history first hand,
Museums and information are there to help you learn about this land.
The winters are strong with lots of snow,
The spring and summer are just right to watch the wheat fields grow.
You will talk about your visit to North Dakota for the rest of your life,
Especially if you visit with your children and you wife.

# ODE TO LEONARD CHIDE

There is a rodeo announcer named Chide,
Who makes you feel like you are part of the ride.
As the bareback rider's head hits the horse's rump,
He makes you grab your head and feel for the lump.
His description of the roping events is a true delight,
You can actually feel the rope going around you tight.
His description of the Saddle Bronc event brings tears to your eyes,
As you feel the pain and see the bruises, no lie.
As he tells of the gracefulness of the barrel riders moves,
You are taken to another place as beautiful as the Louvre.
Then his voice changes to match the mood of the bulls as they through the air fly,
As the rider goes even higher, you can feel the air below and ask yourself; WHY.
When you have had the privilege of listening to rodeo announcer Leonard Chide talk,
You know that you have heard the best and afterwards you will a little higher walk.
If you desire his services, Las Vegas, Nevada is his home,
His love for the Rodeo and entertaining the fans makes him more than willing to roam.

# Off Limits

She lay down beside him in the hay,
He wanted to have her in the worst way.
They rolled back and forth together,
There were holes in the barns roof so they had to watch the weather.
His hands worked on the buttons on her dress,
Her body against his did harder press.
They were down to his shorts and her panties and bra,
When a light showed the shotgun held by her pa.
His words were clear "Son, if you draw water from that well",
"you better be prepared to visit hell.".
The boy left his clothes and bolted across the valley,
That was the closest anybody got to Old Maid Sally.

# One Kings Place

One Kings Place is the place to be,
If you are fortunate to be a Safe Security employee.
There are five Safe Security positions at One Kings Place,
The nature of the positions can keep you at a fast pace.
Main Gate must ensure that no unauthorized individuals the gate hop,
Lobby must ensure that the elevator to the correct unit does stop.
Patrol covers many areas inside and outside to ensure the residents will be secure all day,
Shift Supervisor makes sure the Safe Security employees are following policies in every way.
Last and most important is the Post Commander big and bold,
It is their job to ensure the client stays happy and the relationship does not turn cold.
The residents of One Kings Place deserve security and customer service from the best,
Safe Security employees ensure that they get better service than the rest.

# Opening the Car Door

The young people today are lost,
They do it the lazy way no matter the cost.
Yesterday his car remote went dead,
He was in trouble when he had to use his head.
The hundred dollar mechanic asked him for his keys,
With the keys in his hand he unlocked the door with ease.
The young man said "I did not know that",
The mechanic knew then the young man was a spoiled brat.

# Our Mom

She grew up on a farm on the North Dakota plains,
Flatland used to grow wheat when it rains.
There were her parents and eight siblings to do the work every day,
They used horses and a wagon to haul the fresh cut hay.
The winters were fierce every year,
To survive in the winter they had to wear special gear.
Some years the snow was higher than the doors,
They had to take turns shoveling to see daylight which was quite a chore.
Most of the winter there was a rope from the house to the barn,
So in a blizzard they could find their way without harm.
As the children grew into adults they left the farm to roam,
Some left sooner than others who choose to stay around home.
One brother was short to live,
Brain cancer at 17; death at 19, cut his life to short but he still did a lot give.
She left the farm in 1948 to work at the Variety store in town,
There she met a man who was funny like a clown.
She worked in town or lived on the farm until her marriage in 1951,
A son was born on her first anniversary; he was a lot of fun.
She and her family moved around many times until 1974,
By then they were in Denver and she said no more.
By this time her two sons were under Army rule,
Her two daughters were still in school.
Alcohol had always had a place in her family's life,
As in many families it also caused a lot of strife.
She has been a loving, caring woman all her life,
She also did her best to be a good wife.
At the age of 81, her health is slowly bringing her down,
Luckily for her children she plans on being for a long time around.
This poem from her children is filled with everlasting love,
Their love will continue to engulf her heart like a soft leather glove.

# Outhouse and Pee Pot

## Outhouse

I remember well; visiting relatives and friends on the farm,
There were many things to do but you had to watch for those that could cause harm.
Two things always come to mind, outhouses and pee pots help when you are in a bind,
When you really had to go; you tried to run a short line.
With the outhouse 100 feet from the house,
If you had to sit down to go, you left the house for the outhouse quiet as a mouse.
Once outside you ran real fast; only to get there and it was full,
Wait; it is a two holer, can I come in quick and that is no bull.
Whether it was great-uncle Ole or uncle Sven it did not matter,
Sometimes though it was harder to fit if it was my cousin Jerry who was fatter.

## Pee Pots

At night when us males stand up to go,
We used a pee pot in the closet for our flow.
The pee pot was a large pot with a cover on it,
As much as we hated to go all the way to the outhouse, we could not on it sit.
The pee pot was half filled with water,
It could also be used by the farmer's daughter.
Every morning it was emptied and cleaned,
Afterwards the inside and outside gleaned.
At the time, to use these two items felt like a pain,
The memories are cherished now; even not getting to the outhouse without a stain.

# Owning a Horse

It is a dream of most boys and girls to own a horse someday,
They keep begging their parents in the worst way.
A horse is not something you just buy,
If not taken care of right; when they die you will cry.
I once heard a person say "We are going to do that horse thing.".
I knew right then that any horse they bought, the death bells will ring.
A very serious problem for a horse is called colic.
It causes their intestines to twist and they cannot frolic.
A horse can bring much joy to a person's life,
It is something to do for both a husband and his wife.

# Palm Trees

The palm tree is thirty feet tall,
In a 50 MPH wind it refuses to fall.
This is surprising for the root base is not deep,
This makes it harder to stand on a slope that is steep.
The root base is large just below the ground,
This is the reason so many are still around.
When trimmed properly they can last 100 years,
When one finally falls it can bring a lot of tears.
There are many types of palm trees that grace this land,
On a landscaped property you can see many in one stand.
They can really dress up your yard,
If you don't faint after getting the bill for your credit card.

# Perfect

Hair like silk,
Skin like milk.
Eyes blue bright,
Nose beautiful in the light.
Ears just fine,
Lips; wish they were mine.
Chin with a cute dimple,
Overall very simple.
Neck so cute,
Shoulders not like a brute.
Breast for to die,
Stomach for to cry.
Legs so long and slender,
Feet that completes the member.

# Pontiac

Pontiac was a horse that could easily win First Place,
In all the Horse Show events, but not the race.
He was easy to get in the out of the truck,
Before you could ride him in the events he had to buck.
This also happened each morning on the farm,
Luckily nobody ever got harmed.
When the children moved away from home,
Pontiac was left in the pasture to roam.
The Rodeo Contractor came to the farm one day,
He bought Pontiac for rodeo stock and was on his way.

# Protecting My Home

The doorbell rang late at night,
The broken stillness gave me quite a fright.
I looked through the peephole, but did not see anything,
I jumped back when again the doorbell did ring.
I heard voices talking real low,
About going around to the back door real slow,
At this point I started to get the chills,
I hoped they were inept at their burglary skills.
I retrieved my Bersa Thunder 380 gun,
If I have to, they will not survive to run.
I heard the screen door in the back moving around,
I was hoping the unlocked window was not found.
I decided to try and scare them away,
If they are not scared then they will have to pay.
The last thing I want to do is fire this gun,
Hopefully when they see it they will run.
My wife is upstairs and has called 911,
I can tell you one thing brother, this is no fun.
I decided to push the issue,
Hopefully, the result would not require any tissues.
I looked through the shades and saw the top of his head,
Another one was coming towards the house from the shed.
I pointed the gun at his forehead through the glass,
When he looked up and saw the gun he fell back on his ass.
They both cleared the back wall with ease,
The police did both of them quickly cease.
I was ready to protect my home,
Hopefully they will not for a long time roam.

# Rattlesnake Roundup

To San Saba we went one day,
Driving through the beautiful Texas country side all the way.
The Rattlesnake Roundup today was there,
How they found so many rattlesnakes I know not where.
Some were small and some were very large in size,
To catch them without getting bitten you had to be wise.
The multiple bins were filled with snakes about two feet high,
The reason people would want to catch them I know not why.
They say the meat and skins bring quite a price,
I wonder if the meat tastes good with rice.
The farmers market is there once a month for all,
If you don't want to go alone give somebody a call.
Going to the farmers market was a treat,
There were so many nice people to greet.
The rattlesnake roundup made it a special trip for some,
If you weren't one of those that drank too much rum.

# Revenge

He was walking through the woods in the dark,
He had decided to go this way on a lark.
All of a sudden there were six women around him,
Though a little heavy; surrounded by these women made him feel slim.
He recognized two of them as ones he had made sexual advances to,
About this time he felt he really needed a Lu (bathroom).
He ducked under the first bat but the second one hit him in the head,
He could feel his scalp rip and the blood running red.
He tried to stay on his feet,
But soon found himself on his seat.
The kicks came fast to his arms, chest, legs and groin,
With the many kicks he figured there was damage to parts of his loin.
He thought it was over when suddenly he lost two teeth,
He started to wonder what they would buy for a wreath.
When the police found him he was mumbling about a bat wielding bear,
The police had a hard time from laughing or looking like they cared.

# Rob and Nicole

Wisconsin is the place that they love to call home,
If they leave it is only for a short time to roam.
Brookfield is where Nicole grew up to be as lovely a lady as can,
Waukesha is where Rob's family raised him to be a good man.
Rob decided that being a fireman would be his vocation in life,
To help him share that life, Nicole agreed to be his beautiful wife.
Nicole works in sales but her pets are what fill her mind,
Three dogs and three cats made up of breeds of many kinds.
Bosco, Cana and Ryder are the three dog's names,
Deacon, Ajax and Wasabi are the three cats who play many games.
Nicole spends her time training dogs and taking them to shows,
When Nicole thinks and talks about these times her face just glows.
She also loves to work in the garden and the contortions of yoga for a while,
The fruits of things she has grown and her yoga exercise make her smile.
Rob is one of the few in the world, who put their life on the line every day,
To make sure his friends, neighbors and others feel safe in his own way.
When off duty he loves to watch the Packers with his friend Old Jack No. 7,
Boy; watching the Packers win and spending time with Jack is like heaven.
Rob also uses his knowledge to bring in extra income with his business "Get Lit",
When installing or repairing an electrical problem he must keep all his wit.
The Honda S2000 that Rob speeds around in when the roads are dry,
Is so exhilarating that his heartbeat quickens and people wonder why.
If you've ever had a chance to drive this exceptional vehicle even once very far,
You will know for yourself why Rob holds his head higher while driving this car.
This poem is from a friend about Rob and Nicole,
They will be there when you need them down in your soul.

# Sawyer Fincher

Sawyer came into our lives while still in his mother's womb,
Jill was very pregnant and had trouble using a broom.
Jill stayed with us until Shannon arrived,
I learned not to get between a pregnant lady and food if you want to stay alive.
Sawyer was born healthy with ten fingers and ten toes,
I bought him clothes for a three year old after searching through the clothes in rows.
If it was cute to my eye, I did it buy,
My wife Sandy would give me that "you're hopeless" look and that is not a lie.
He joined the living on May 10, 2007,
God was looking down on us with pride from Heaven.
From three months to three years his presence graced our home during the day,
He brought a special love to us in his own way.
As he grew, so did our love for him,
Over this time he became tall and slim.
His intellect was always high,
He could entertain himself for hours playing, waiting for the grilled cheese to fry.
Lives journey had not allowed us in the past to share our own love this special way,
He attends preschool now during the day.
Our time with him is a lot less than before,
This makes the time we did spend with him special as we played on the floor.
It tugs at our hearts when he hugs our leg and says "I Love You",
Our moving away and not seeing him as often will definitely make us blue.
We will cherish the memories of our time around him in the past,
Nobody can take them away from us until we breathe our last.
Each time we see him in the future we will feel our best,
We know he will grow up to be better than the rest.
His great-uncle and great-aunt will always have a special place in their hearts for him,
We know he will grow up to be handsome and slim.

# Selma Sikes

This poem is for a beautiful lady named Selma Sikes,
Different in her own and special way, Oh Yikes.
This poem only covers certain things about her life,
A life that has been full of many good things, but also sorrow and strife.
This poem was written by a good friend named Dan Noss,
Who if with his wife Sandy had not met Selma they would have been at a loss.
She was raised in a life of affluence and glamour in Beverly Hills,
But her personality kept her feet on the ground and gave her a strong will.
She married David Sikes, who was her soul mate to be for life,
Their daughter Selma Josephine made her a very happy mother and wife.
At a time when David and she felt that California was in the past,
They moved to Las Vegas, Nevada and bought a home that was to be their last.
In December 2004, God decided it was time to bring David home,
A tragic event that stunned Selma to her sole, though she knows she is never alone.
She had to rely on her personality and strong will to survive,
But with the support of her friends and the Lord the time to continue her life had arrived.
Selma is excited about Peter and Selma Josephine's upcoming baby boy,
A baby that will continue David's legacy with much love and joy.

# Selma Sikes Birthday

Selma Sikes is a fox,
Just watch the way she rocks.
Another birthday is passing her way,
But she is still in love with life as with any other day.
The birthdays fly by, 40s, 50s 60 . . . . ish they go,
But she is still beautiful from head to toe.
Her friendship is special to whoever she knows,
If there is anybody who doesn't think so, that is how life goes.
Happy 60ish birthday to our special friend today,
It is 6 days early but it doesn't matter anyway.

# Sexual Needs

Every person has different sexual needs,
Some are basic and others are exotic like in the weeds.
Some can wait a while; while others desire multiple sessions every day,
Those who require multiple sessions have to worry about their partners in many ways.
Ones that wait a while must be careful when they select a partner for their thriller,
One partner or many does not matter; disease is an equal opportunity killer.
Statistics say that normal sexual sessions are three times a week,
Those who require multiple sessions; do constantly partners seek.
Either category you fall into is not wrong,
If you are in the multiple sessions category; your heart better be strong.
There are some that are married and count years instead of days,
They try to be creative to get those years converted to days in many ways.

# Short

Short people put up with issues other people don't,
It is not that they cannot do other things or won't.
In a crowd they always end up in the back,
In a store they are always given the biggest sack.
Every house is made for everybody taller,
They have to be creative or give somebody a holler,
They are smart people that do not let most things stop them for long,
They know what things they need to do and when and are never wrong.
Just because they are born of smaller stature than others,
They are all loved dearly by their mother.

# Short Pig Tale

The pig fell in the mud,
He still could not get off the crud.
The mud kept him cool,
He hates a clean water pool.
He loves to eat all day,
He can get big and fat that way.
Why is he (farmer) giving me (pig) that eye,
Probably tomorrow I will be bacon to fry.

# Short Sale

We work hard all our life,
Hoping to not go through much strife.
Then one day our quiet world tumbled down,
For no reason of our own, our life as it was; is no where around.
As a family, we cut back everywhere we can,
When our income drops up to 80%, we quickly feel the heat of the frying pan.
Our current assets prohibit a government savior plan (LOL) as glue,
We talk to the lawyers and a short sale is all we can do.
We can also walk away (foreclosure),
But it will bother us until our dying day.
For most short sales; we must stop paying the bank,
On a scale of our morals, that does very low rank.
The bank wants us to give our last penny to them,
We are already losing everything we have worked for; they could care less when.
When we have never missed a payment; it mentally is a pain,
We feel like every day from now on will be full of rain.
Missing the first payment is the hardest,
Time will only tell if it was the smartest.
A lawyer is the best way for a short sale to go,
They know how to talk to the bank and keep everything on an even flow.
The application, negotiation and decision can kill a faint heart,
We are sure for some marriages it even tears them a part.
If everything finally goes through and we can breathe a sigh of relief,
We have to start over like 30 years ago stunned in our belief.
Even though our face will have a frown,
We know that the bad guys will never get us down

# Shorty

Shorty was a small horse with a Texas sized heart,
Like all horses he would like to fart.
We would bring him to our backyard to play,
He would eat the grass but he preferred hay.
The Saddle Club arena was on top of the hill,
You could hear them, if you were still.
Shorty loved Tuesday nights the most,
I would saddle him and then hitch him to a post.
I would ride him to the saddle club for events at night,
Shorty was always ready to give it a good fight.
The thoroughbreds were taller and faster than him,
But even though Shorty never won; his time behind them was slim.
In team penning Shorty was the best,
A calf never got past him like some of the rest.
Shorty showed those thoroughbreds his heart was bigger than most,
I am sure now in horse heaven he is greeting them all as their host.

# Single in 2010 (Male)

Most of what my dad told me about him dating my mom does not pertain now,
At first I tried to follow his words and boy; POW.
Women in 2010 are so much different than before,
I am not saying that is wrong; it is that I must learn a lot more.
In my father's era few women worked outside the home,
In 2010 women know what they want when they roam.
You cannot assume anything about women now,
If you do they will quickly put you in your place; and how.
You must take it slow at first,
If you go to fast you can make it worse.
Some women want to be treated like a princess every day,
Others will drink you under the table and in bed twist you many ways.
You have to learn to go with the flow,
You must take your time finding out what makes them glow.
Doris Day (you remember her; right) said it best when she sang "What will be, will be',
In 2010 dating can be a he and she, or she and she, or he and he.

# Sisters

Sisters have a very special bond much different than brothers,
Their affection can come to the point they feel smothered.
Sisters can talk to each other every day,
They can still come up with new exciting things by the way.
They confide more things between them than the weaker sex,
They keep track of things in a book of text.
There isn't much more to say about this matter,
It would only be more spectacular chatter.

# Skin Deep

She was not the best looking girl in the school,
Everybody always teased her and called her a fool.
They bullied her all day long,
Their meanness would not let them believe it was wrong.
She learned to accept the verbal abuse,
When they continued on to the Internet there was no excuse.
The things they put on the Internet got worse all a long,
She could not take it anymore and contacted the Police who said that they were wrong.
They did not think they were smart when they got arrested,
Then they found out that the charges could not be contested.
They thought that because they were pretty and she was not; it was all right,
What they did not realize is that there is more to a person than what is in sight.

# Sky Diving Experience

As she steps out into the morning breeze,
Her eyes caught the gentle waves of the seas.
This is the day that she has been waiting for,
The thought of floating through the air excites her even more.
She had dreamed about skydiving for a long time,
But she had to wait because this sport can cost a pretty dime.
As she approached the small air strip,
She started to remember her friends tip.
Only fools jump out of a perfectly good airplane at 2,000 feet,
She knew that this was a joke, but was determined to this meet.
A one hour class and the perfect landing form helped to show the way,
Would help her know what would be expected on this special day.
When her name was called to put on her chute and head for the plane,
She tried to hide such thoughts as "hopefully it will rain".
When the chute was fully installed and felt really tight,
As she had trouble walking to the plane, was the chute installed right.
As the plane took off and climbed high in the air,
She and the other person really looked like a scared pair.
As the jump master opened the door and said "are you ready to go",
She nodded her head yes, even though inside she was screaming "no".
As she stepped out of the plane, the wing strut she did hold,
The feeling of joy that ran through her stopped the feeling of the metal so cold.

As she let go and the breath from her body did leave,
Please open chute so my family won't need to grieve.
Before she could think, the chute opened and she was jerked to the core,
Now she knew why making sure the chute was tight was a chore.
As she breathed again and looked across the sky,
She knew that never again would she say, skydive, WHY?
Her euphoria was broken by the radio saying left riser or right,
She then remembered that to steer; pull one of the risers tight.
To soon the joy of floating through the air came to a stop,
As she realized how fast towards the ground she did drop.
She pulled first on the left riser and then the right to go back,
To the proper landing location and not end up in the hay stack.
Just before the ground she pulls hard on both risers to slow her speed,
To ensure that of her hospital visit they would not in the paper read.
As she picked herself up off the ground after receiving a little bump,
She was full of pride and joy as she prepared to make another jump.

# Sniper

The sniper stayed froze in position for hours,
After two weeks in the field he really needed a shower.
All he needed to do his job,
Was a one square inch target for a life to rob,
The terrorists had been hiding here for years,
To kill them; his job would not bring any tears.
He saw a movement and tensed for a shot,
His shot shattered the man's skull and all that was left would rot.
There was noise and movement as they looked at their comrade's blood,
They knew to not be exposed or there would be a red flood.
They would never find his place,
From 1500 yards he had shattered the man's face.
He knew they would stay by the shelter for peace of mind,
Now the Air Force could kill them all as they hid behind their fake blind.

# Snow Skiing

Three feet from the chalet I did almost fall,
I would have except for the wall.
I made it to the ski lift in one piece.
When I got to the top I did not want to release.
After my death grip was broken,
I realized that I was their sacrifice token.
The beginners slope was not at the top,
What I saw was a big, big drop.
I tried to snowplow but the hill was to steep,
Believe me I found out that the snow was deep.
After thirty minutes and a sore ankle bone,
I realized these were not my problems alone.
Near the bottom I decided to straighten out,
I got going so fast I could not even shout.
All of a sudden I was in the air from a bump,
When I landed I did not move from the hole under my rump.
Eventually I moved my hands and toes,
I was glad when they did not have any holes.
The next time we went snow skiing I stayed in the lodge,
With a beer in my hand I did the snow monster dodge.

# Snowshoeing on Mount Charleston

Shannon and Jill drove up the mountain,
Looking for the snow throwing fountain.
To snowshoe was their quest,
They practiced and practiced to be their best.
Little Sawyer with Aunie Hany (Sawyer talk for Aunt Sandy) were at home,
Waiting for the day when he to can roam.
They start up the mountain in snowshoes with ease,
They found the trek harder when they felt the breeze.
As the breeze got stronger they felt the distain,
To their objective a long distance did remain.
They made it to the spot where they wanted to turn around,
The breeze and snow were now coming down,
They started back down when they found,
They were cold and their car was far below upon the ground.
They both gave a sigh,
"Boy; are we up high".
The eagle from its nest below them flew,
Their snowshoes against the snow felt like glue.
The downhill trek to the car was long,
Their bodies told them; boy this was wrong.
When they finally got back to the house,
They both felt as weak as a mouse.
The next time that Shannon and Jill drove up the mountain,
They could not find the snow throwing fountain.
They could only find the sun's ray,
They drove back home to their dismay.
Sawyer, Dan and Sandy were there with the grill hot.
They all enjoyed a barbeque where everyone ate a lot.

# South Dakota

South Dakota is the place you aut to be,
It is a beautiful part of the land of the free.
The east side is flat with pheasants and corn for all to see,
The west side has the Black Hills seen personally by me.
Rodeo is a large part of living there,
On most weekends you can attend one anywhere,
Some of the best cowboys in the world live in this state,
When it comes to rodeo cowboys South Dakota is 1st rate.
The Corn Palace in Mitchell is one of a kind,
The changing beauty of it every year will blow your mind.
The three day rodeo in Belle Fourche in July is a special event,
You will think that the rodeos and parade were heaven sent.
If you ever need a place to get away,
South Dakota is the place to stay.

# Special Love

It takes a strong and loving woman to raise two children alone,
She brought these children from a society where lack of care will chill you to the bone.
Many trips to China made her dreams come true by two,
She loves them so much she wants to keep them close with glue.
One is growing into a beautiful young woman before her sight,
The other one will always be her little girl; you got that right.
She struggles in life to give them a safe and happy home,
But she also knows that as life goes on they will want to roam.
This woman's name is Carrie,
An even with lives tribulations it is hard to not see her merry.
Caitlan was the first to grace her life years ago,
She adopted Caitlan even though the process was slow.
Later she opened her heart again to Julia, a beautiful young girl,
As she grew up she bounced around like a squirrel.
When you see these three together their love for each other will make you cry,
If you wonder what makes a woman alone adopt two girls, the above phrase explains why.
As her two daughters grow older they will eventually move away,
They have the life they were given and they will not be able to stay.
There are two times each when Carrie's tears will flow; college and marriage,
She will be busting with joy as they both pull up to a church in a white carriage.
As Carrie gets older with a few hairs of gray,
She will have her grandchildren with which to play.
When she gets really old she will have many fond memories to remember,
The loving life she gave these two girls from China will be repaid during her December.
Sometime in the future when she is called to sit by the Lords side,
She will be able to look down on her two girls and smile with pride.

Dedicated to my close friend and exceptional lady Carrie Bertram.

# Strange Homecoming

He was listed as a POW/MIA for years,
His family had shed a million tears.
His family forced themselves to move on,
They did not want to; but had to believe he was gone.
They had no way to know,
That 30 years later he would show.
They did not know the man who stood before them now,
He did look a little familiar but they could not tell how.
They all talked for a while and they asked if he could a little longer stay,
He said he knew they all had new lives and he had to be on his way.

# Susan Bach

This poem is about a special lady named Susan Bach,
Who as a Daughter, Wife, and Mother is solid as a rock.
Growing up in a large and loving family in Wisconsin was a joy,
With her husband Woody two daughters did they have; oh boy.
Their Harley Davidson hog brought them many, many good times,
Down the highway they would fly; bugs in their teeth and hair full of grime.
Health problems as age crept up on them slowed them down a little; NOT,
They decided to trade Wisconsin for the lights of Las Vegas; but oh so hot.
At a Catholic School is where to teach she did choose,
Susan decided to teach one of the third grade classes; they did not lose.
Susan's life was dealt a most devastating blow while in Wisconsin one summer day,
When the Lord decided to bring Woody home; to stand beside him always.
The loss of her beloved Woody left her feeling stripped to the bone,
But having family close by at this time of need gave her strength to go on.
Susan returned to Las Vegas to continue her life with cats Bully and It,
Woody is always close by watching Television with his same wit.
Visits from family and friends helped tremendously to ease some of the pain,
But wouldn't you know it the days her family visited; Las Vegas was full of rain.
Pain of this intensity takes a long time but totally never subsides,
Especially the remembrance and joy of the Harley Davidson rides.
The day that the Harley Davidson to North Dakota moved away,
The tearful finality of this event sneaks into her memory every day.
Susan's strong Wisconsin personality brightens everybody's life,
If only the Ford Pickup truck would run better and give her less strife.
Her friends in Las Vegas have her in their thoughts every day,
As this special lady continues on life's way.

# Tall

Tall people put up with issues other people don't,
It is not that they cannot do other things or won't.
In a crowd they always end up in the front,
When it comes to basketball they are asked to do stunts.
Every house is made for somebody shorter,
They swear they are built low with less mortar.
They are smart people, who do not let most things bother them for long,
They know what things they need to do and when and are never wrong.
Just because they are born of taller stature than others,
They are all loved dearly by their mother.

## Tatonka (Buffalo)

Tatonka, the life blood of the Indian's life,
When Tatonka is scare they have a lot of strife.
They use every part to survive,
There is much joy when Tatonka arrives.
The skin in tanned and used in many ways,
It keeps them warm on cold nights and days.
The meat is used to keep their stomachs full,
To get some meat to eat they would pull.
The bones were used for weapons and tools,
When it came to what they could make there was not any rules.
They used the stomach, intestines and brains to,
These parts would make a very good stew.
When the Indians kill Tatonka there is no waste,
The whites left the meat to rot instead of taste.
The whites hunting almost brought Tatonka down to zero,
Sadly in this part of history there are not any heroes.
As the number of Tatonka got less and less,
The Indians were in an awful mess.
When Tatonka was gone from their sight,
They knew that their end was not right.
Today many Indians have forgotten what Tatonka meant to their lives,
They live in a white man's world that cuts them deep like many knives.

# Tattoos

Some think that Tattoos look good,
Others think you came from the hood.
You can show your moms or girl's name,
You can have two or three the same.
Some colors from the past are bright,
Many of the current colors are out-of-sight.
Some tattoos are small and neat,
Some cover your whole back and onto your seat.
Your individuality is shown to all,
You can show more individuality when you are tall.
You can let your imagination go wild,
You can also decide to be mild.
Many businesses' today do not want any tattoos to show,
The extra clothes make it miserable when the temperature is not low.
In the year 2010 tattoos are not as accepted as they used to be,
It seems like tattoos are more acceptable on a he than a she.
I have two tattoos myself and thought of getting more,
Then my wife asked me if I wanted to wash up on the shore.
Getting a tattoo is using your body as a canvas; sometimes for love,
You can also use your canvas to show your love for the Lord above.
This poem could go on forever for tattoo designs will never end,
Only when your imagination dies, will your brain no longer designs send.

# The Ammo Dump

Their assignment was to blow up the ammo dump,
The guards were to be killed and everything left in a clump.
They parachuted in two miles from there,
They closed in on the guards as if to come from nowhere.
There were four guards and the first two died quick,
The third one was dead before he hit the ground, his throat pierced by a stick.
Near the fourth guard's position they could set the charge without being seen,
They left enough cord to get away, this assignment had been clean.
As the ammo dump exploded the fourth guard never knew what hit him,
They were far enough away that their chances of getting caught were slim.
The satellite map showed the enemy had lost six months of ammo supplies,
A job well done was one of the General's replies.

# The Back Gate

Some nights I am assigned to the Back Gate,
I always wonder what will be my fate.
From midnight to light everything is very dark,
To the guard house, I very close my car park.
It is so quiet every sound is loud to me,
The small guard house get smaller and I want to get free.
The creatures from the golf course sometimes come by,
The only one that I care to see is the fly,
The rabbits scratch at the door,
The spiders make me keep my feet off the floor.
The night the coyote looks in the window at me,
My backside running down the street is all you will see.

# The Boyfriend's View

The other day my girlfriend told me she was not happy,
She said her breasts were too small and flappy.
She wanted them enlarged but not much,
She showed me a picture saying as such.
She made an appointment for next week,
She told me I would get the first peek.
The procedure went well,
By the smile on her face I could tell.
I was happy with her looks before,
Now I was happy even more.
I did my best to help massage them with care,
The best part was seeing her bare.
When she is happy, so am I,
They are now really nice; no lie.

# The Buffalo Ranch

I know of a Buffalo Ranch in South Dakota that the buffalo call home,
It is on land where the Sioux Indians used to roam.
You can see the butte where the Indians chased the buffalo over; in their special way.
They would kill only enough buffalo to survive the cold winter days.
The Limpert Buffalo Ranch is a beautiful place to be,
They have 5,000 buffalo on 20,000 acres; you see.
You cannot herd buffalo like you do cows,
Or chase them into a pen like you do sows.
They know that they rule the range all the time,
If you try to herd them all you will do is whine.
There is a feed called candy that is sweet to the taste,
The Buffalo will follow the trail but not in a haste.
Throughout the year they are brought in and put in large pens,
They are given vaccinations and mingle with wild turkey hens.
Technology has allowed them to create new products to sell,
Fertilizer from the manure; hopefully the prices have not fell.
Working these majestic wild beasts everyday is always tough,
If you get in a situation where you are vulnerable, it can get rough.
ATVs were used to try to move them around the range,
One day a bull out ran the ATV and flipped it and the rider causing a change.
Now they use motorcycles for this which gives them more speed,
You still cannot make them come like this because you cannot lead.
The feeling of being two feet from these majestic beasts is a thrill,
With the vehicle door between you and them you are safe but it can give you a chill.
Across the United States there are plenty of places where you can buffalo see,
The Limpert Buffalo Ranch in northwestern South Dakota is very special to me.

# The Bus

Leaving Dhahran during Desert Shield,
We have to be ready for whatever the enemy wields.
On a bus is not a safe place to be,
If the enemy attacked; it is easy to see.
To make sure that you come out alive,
You have to be ready if the enemy arrives.
If the enemy makes the bus stop,
Everybody must to their positions hop.
The soldiers in the middle will provide cover fire,
While those in the front and the back depart like a live wire.
As they hit the ground they fall and roll,
Hopefully they can hide behind a shrub or a pole.
They roll to get farther away,
Because it is certain death if they stay.
When all are off the bus and on the ground,
The ranking officer evaluates the attack and starts checking around.
He identified a triage area for the hurt,
As the attack subsides the soldiers build protection with dirt.
The scouts returned and said the enemy had moved off,
The ranking officer gets everybody on the bus moving very soft.
The bus started fast and moved on down the road,
They had weathered the attack well following the soldiers code.
To this day the attack is stuck in their minds,
As they think of other battles of many kinds.
Whatever your job is you're a soldier first,
Many of them knew from that day; they had been destined to be soldiers from birth.

# The Camera

I am a camera who can create memories when used with skill,
Many times though I shutter (no pun intended) at the pictures I take and get the chills.
How come I am forced to take butt and bathroom shots,
I cost people big money to be abused a lot.
When it is a picture I do not want to take,
I make it fuzzy or black out the photo to make,
I am dropped, kicked and banged around,
I am cussed at when later the photo cannot be found.
Sometimes I get to take photos of babies,
Then I am forced to take pictures of naked ladies.
I have many advanced features,
To use them all, my owner needs a teacher.
All I ask for is a little tender care,
You will not believe the beautiful photos I will share.
I have seen things that would make you cry,
One thing about me is that I do not lie.
I can be around for many years,
Over that time I will show you photos that will bring you to tears.
What; you bought another camera to replace me,
I suppose it has even more features you cannot use without a fee.
Please give me to somebody where I will have a loving home,
I do not want to sit in a dark place all alone.

# The Chair

Listening to my favorite songs on the radio today makes me cry,
This was the last time to hear these songs before it is my time to fry.
I faintly remember so long ago what happened for which I must die.
At my trial they said that I took four innocent lives and this I could not deny.
My mind has seemed to blank out this terrible crime,
At that point in my life I was in my prime.
I remember my partner saying that this is an easy way to make money,
Now her husband will never again get to hear her call him honey.
Two of the three others were also a partner of a marriage.
I ended their lives before they could push a baby carriage.
They say that the electric force of the chair will end my life in a hurry,
I hope that the Lord has forgiven me for what happened in a flurry.
I hear them coming to get me as they are ringing a bell,
I asked my friend to play his guitar for me as I pass his cell.
As they strap me arms, legs and head to the chair,
I am frightened but I know that for what I done this is only fair.
When they opened the curtain I did not see one person related to me,
I was told they are my victim's relatives who chose to come and see.
Tears came to my eyes as I mouthed "I'm sorry" to them,
I looked at the man with his hand on the switch; his expression did not say when.
As I saw his muscles tense I knew the end was here,
Thank you Lord for now I have nothing more to fear.

# The Church and the Devil

Many people think that the Church is fine,
Even a few of them say the Church is mine.
Some Priests and Administrators think they are above the rest,
But they will always fail the test.
Some of them at the top,
Think that everybody below them should hop.
Those at the top think that they are always right,
But they are so far in the dark that they will never see the light.
They hide their true identity behind a religious cause,
They think that they are above the Christian laws.
When the holier than thou wears off, the true color of the Devil comes to be,
No matter whether the Devil is a she or a he.
They will use all evil ways known to man,
They try to find even more evil ways if they can.
There are also wannabes, who behind the Devil tag along,
They don't care if what they do is religiously wrong.
The feeling of POWER engulfs them to the core,
The Devil in them will use whatever to push good people out the door.

# The Cold War

The year was 1977 and the Cold War was in full swing,
My Army unit from Kitzingen, West Germany thought a border tour was the thing.
The Army organization guarding the East Germany border was a long way from home,
We stopped close to the Iron Curtin about twenty feet away as we were shown.
Next we stopped across the river from a large town,
The Iron Curtain across the middle of the bridge was easily found.
Not one person could be seen on the East Germany side,
They did not have anything but a bicycle to ride.
They had to first call the East Germany Police before going to the store,
If they came out of their yard without permission, it probably would have looked like war.
They again had to call the East Germany Police the minute they got to the store,
This played out every time they wanted to leave their yard for places to go more.
There were East Germany guards that watched the river and the bridge,
It was summer but on the East Germany side you could almost feel the frost like from a fridge.
You had to prove your loyalty to East Germany before you could live this close to the border,
If you thought about escaping to West Germany, you would meet dogs, rifle fire and mortars.
Thank God in 1989 the Iron Curtain and the Berlin Wall were no more to be,
If you make a trip to this village today, freedom will be there for as far as you can see.

# The Cowboys Winning Ride

He looked at the bulls in the chutes,
As he looked, he could feel a deep shaking down in his boots.
He knew that it would soon be his time to ride,
He kept his lucky charm close by his side.
He headed for chute number four,
He wished that he had practiced more.
The bull's eyes were glazed,
He knew that this ride would all amaze.
In getting settled on the bull, he pulled his rope tight,
He hoped that for this ride he had it just right.
As he signaled for the gate and the bull burst out of the chute,
He could feel that this ride would bring him a lot of loot.
The bull went into a spin the speed of lightening,
The cowboy could feel the muscles by his stomach tightening.
As the eight second horn sounded ending the ride,
He knew that the Lord was on his side.
He knew that the dismount was the time to fear,
A hoof on bone is the last thing he wanted to hear.
He separated from the bull in a flash,
He was glad that the dirt would not leave a rash.
As he hit the ground,
Boy; did his head pound.
The cowboy got up off the ground,
He knew that he had won this round.
The bull looked at the cowboy with a smirk on his face,
That beamed; let's see who wins the next eight second race.
The bull and the cowboy put on a good show,
The fans knew they would have a memory that would not let go.

# A Dolphins Life

The mother dolphin swam with her calf by her side,
Sometimes the calf would even hitch a ride.
They glided through the water with grace and completely silent,
This is in contrast with the shark who is usually violent.
The dolphin's migration path is very long,
Their supreme navigational skills ensured that the path is never wrong.
They attached themselves to a pod of dolphins, some with calves along,
The chorus they all created made for a beautiful song.
As they met up with tourist vessels on the way,
They could tell that they gave the tourists a special day.
The water changed colors from shallow to deep,
Their anxiety to get to their destination would not let them sleep.
Along the way a few calves were lost,
Even though the mothers tried to save them at any cost.
They finally made it to their winter grounds,
When mating started, the mothers would again add pounds.
As the calves inside them grew larger by the day,
The calves born last year did not travel far away.
By the time the mothers started their migration back to give birth,
They would travel a little slower because of their increased girth.
Last year's calves followed along on the migration for two more years,
When it was time to leave their mothers, I'd swear I could see some tears.
This migration has gone on for centuries to bring new life,
It will continue whether or not man causes strife.
Watching these beautiful creatures can make a grown person weep,
The troubles of the world seem to disappear when they sleep.

# The Dream

Her breasts rise as they come to life,
If only that would happen with his wife.
Her stomach is flat and her buttocks is round,
His wife's stomach and buttocks are a little more sound.
Her thighs and calves from a goddess come,
His wife's are larger by some.
Her body sends sexy signals when she walks,
His wife could do this but she always talks.
She motions for him to follow behind the door,
At that moment the alarm rings to his horror,
He looks over at this wife's side of the sack,
He caresses her hair that is black.
He remembers the dream as good,
But cheat on his beautiful wife he never would.
His wife awakes and sees his strange stare,
He hugs her close to show her that he cares.

# The Early Adventures of Bogdan Jucan

Bogdan at 20 to the USA came,
He left Romania looking for another game.
He wanted to know what the rest of the world had to give,
He first settled in California where he decided to live.
His determination and desire gave him a start above the rest,
That also put him in a league of the best.
Not all though was a blessing,
A marriage in 2005 kept him guessing.
Later he decided that to Las Vegas he would move,
With the marriage in disarray he would try another groove.
His hard work helped him to two jobs find,
Security and Bail Bonds years earlier probably never came to mind.
In Las Vegas there were many women that wanted to be by his side,
But he met one that he decided he wanted for the long ride.
This poem will stop right here for now,
Check back later to read more about Bogdan's where, when and how.

# The Elk Hunt

Harry was from the city,
He thought that he was pretty witty.
When he first got to the ranch,
He gave everybody the stare and the stance.
Inside he was as scared as a child,
But wanted people to think he was cool and mild.
This was his first Montana elk hunt,
His city slicker friends had put him up to this stunt.
This was his first time out of the city in 20 years,
His friends who had never left the city gave him jeers.
This was his first time in the Montana hills,
The frost in the morning gave him the chills.
He had forgotten how beautiful things were,
Especially in the morning when the animals start to stir.
He saw many animals the first day,
But the majestic elk stood out while eating hay.
The next day he had the large elk in his sight,
But he couldn't pull the trigger, even with all his might.
The next day he had the best time of his life,
Except for the day his true love became his wife.
The pictures he took that day will hang on his wall,
When his new house is completed sometime in the fall.
His city friends said that what he went through sounded like a lot of work,
It was at that time that he realized his city friends were all jerks.
As he plans for his next hunt, this time for a moose,
Using a camera instead of a rifle has turned his free spirit loose.

# The Evil Sheep

A sheepherder was working for his pay,
One day a new sheep came up and asked if he could stay.
The sheepherder said yes wanting to be kind,
The new sheep said thanks knowing that other things were on his mind.
The sheepherder treated the new sheep with loving hands,
As the new sheep started his evil plan.
The new sheep started to spread his dirt,
The sheepherder wanted to believe in the new sheep but was still hurt.
As days go on the new sheep kept causing more tension,
The sheepherder did not want to cause an issue so he this did not mention.
The new sheep's true colors came out as he transformed into a wolf very evil to all,
As a wolf he started his destruction of the herd; the sheepherder knew the wolf had to fall.
The sheepherder watched for his chance and sent the wolf to hell with one shot,
Good will eventually overtake evil for people that believe in the Lord a lot.

# The Family Farm

The farmer wiped his brow and a tear appeared as he sold his last cow,
To make it worse next week he will also have to sell his last sow.
The tractors and baler will be the last items to go,
Since this all started he had never felt so low.
His debits rose quicker than his credits and the end came fast,
He had grown up on this farm and dreaded the day that will be his last,
In 50 years the family farm will be hard to find,
What a family farm was will not be in their mind.
When this day comes it will be sad for all,
Family farms sustained America for decades but nobody will recall.

# The Fawn and the Chipmunk

The world goes round and round,
It is full of beautiful sounds.
The fawn plays in the hay,
He does as he may.
He frolics here and there,
Not caring about why, when or where.
The chipmunk plays in the hay to,
The fawn knows he is not alone, but wonders who.
The fawn is startled when the chipmunk shows his face,
He runs across the field like it is in a race.
His mother was watching from a far,
Intent on protecting him from a car.
The mother with fawn in tow,
Picked the safest way to go.
As the mother and fawn lay down for the night,
The beautiful sounds of the forest make it just right.

# The Final Straw

They had been married for ten years,
Most of them she was in tears.
Her husband charmed her at first,
He started drinking and things went from bad to worse.
He started beating her three times a week,
She was too scared for public help to seek.
She had many hospital visits and denials to the police,
She knew if he went to jail it would be worse upon his release.
She finally decided that she had enough,
The next time he beat her she would get rough.
Two days later he came home drunk,
He had heaved on himself and really stunk.
He reached to embrace her and she slipped away,
He said "I'll kill you and leave you in a field of hay."
She had made her decision in her mind,
She was not going to take another beating of any kind.
His first swing hit her shoulder,
The look in her eyes got ever colder.
He swung again and she ducked under,
Her knife sliced across his stomach, and the blood made him wonder.
He swung again and missed,
She cut him again and he began to list.
He tried to swing again but fell to his knees,
By this time his stomach looked like swiss cheese.
EMS got him to the hospital just in time,
Because of his violent past his wife was not charged with a crime.

# The Flood

The rain started days ago,
At that time the water was low.
The weather man said hold on to your hats,
Head for the attic with the bats.
On the sixth day of steady rain,
The weather man decided to use his brain.
He said the river is going over its banks,
It is at that time our hearts sank.
The water kept rising fast,
We knew the sandbags would not last.
We moved everything into the attic in a hurry,
If the water gets that high it will not pay to worry.
The water slowed but kept creeping,
This is better than at first when it was leaping.
On the ninth day the rain finally stopped,
Everybody was so happy they did the bunny hop.
Our first floor has two inches of water that was bad enough,
For families that lost everything it was really rough.
After many days the river went back to normal,
The government came in and wanted everything formal.
It took two years before everybody's property was neat,
The government was not much help while they sat on their seat.

# The Fly

He sat intensely looking at the screen,
I looked at him and said to myself "lets be mean".
I flew from the ceiling to the wall,
Without a concern because I could not fall.
My plan was to land on his ear,
When he slapped at me I would not fear.
I can see the muscles tense in his neck,
It should not take long to make him a wreck.
Next I landed on his nose,
He swung at me as he rose.
Another left than a right,
I could tell he really wanted to kill me out of spite.
I kept moving just out of his reach,
He was getting so mad it affected his speech.
He is running away,
I knew that he would not stay.
Wait; is that a newspaper he is making into a roll,
At this point my game is over as I alight on top of a pole.

# The Hobo's Tale

The whistle announced the train coming down the track,
The hobo stirred from his makeshift bed by the lumber stack.
The picture of his first hobo ride flashed through his mind,
Not knowing at that time he would travel on trains of many kinds.
He remembers well the faces of his wife and child from ago,
Every time while listening to the rhythm of the rails as he rode below.
He hoped everyday what he did for his family was the best,
While he was riding the rails back and forth across the west.
The year was 1932 when he was forced to look for work away from home,
He did not realize that the years would fly by so fast as he continued to roam.
He was able to get work now and then but the pay was slim,
The job was never long enough to contact his family to join him.
He prayed to God everyday as he rode the rails,
That his family would one day live in a house built of wood and nails.
His final words came one day as the train he was riding on derailed,
A picture and letter in his pocket told the authorities where it should be mailed.
His wife and child felt the sorrow of losing a loving husband and father in May,
But they knew that he was in heaven and waiting to be joined by them one day.

# The Hobo's Wife and Child

It was 1932 and the depression was on,
Her husband had to leave, but did not know how long he would be gone.
The tears flowed freely for her and their child,
As they watched him head for the train knowing it would be dangerous and wild.
The first month for her and the child were full of pain,
To add to this feeling the weather was full of rain.
She anxiously waited everyday for the mail,
She would go to the Post Office even in the middle of the hail.
Her heart dropped every time he said he had to keep looking,
She wished his letters would say "Call the depot for a train ticket booking.
When the letters stopped suddenly she was full of fear,
Not knowing his fate brought back the tears.
The letter about his death from the police in Randall,
Hit her to the core and she did not know how she would this handle.
His body returned home by train one lonely day,
His wife and child walk to the cemetery through beautiful fields of hay.
His love for them had taken him on this path,
Building up in her heart was such a wrath.
They buried him by his parents near the big oak tree,
He is now permanently a part of the land of the free.
For her child's sake she has to go on,
She had to make sure his memory is never gone.

# The Last Ten Feet

My friend pulled into my driveway one night at ten,
I told my wife I would be home; but I cannot remember when.
The door opened and I slid out onto the ground,
Good thing my friend did not charge me by the pound.
The house front door was only ten feet from me,
It should have been easy for me you see.
After getting up my first step was fine,
I was proud of myself for walking a straight line.
The second step did not go so well,
I slipped on the grass and fell.
As I went down I grabbed the cord to the big metal bell,
I am sure the neighborhood wished at that moment I would sell.
Then I figured it was safer to crawl with only four feet to go,
I started crawling up the steps when my hands slipped, oh no.
The next thing I saw was blood on my nose when I hit the step hard,
I fell forward onto the top step like a ton of lard.
I got to my knees and opened the door with luck,
I finally made it in the house without again getting stuck.
When I awoke fully clothed in the tub,
My wife said I smelled; and to first rub.
That last ten feet about done me in,
When you are drunk, you can never win.

# The Legacy of Reverend Law

Reverend Law is the people's preacher,
He raises heaven and lowers hell as a teacher.
Fire and Brimstone everyday is his way,
He never stops firing his words be it night or day.
A little corn squeezins each morning always brings,
The beautiful words that from his mouth sings.
His calling takes him from town to town,
But in the 1880's it was a struggle to get around.
His horse is travel worn and his saddle is to,
But his faith in the Lord would not let him be blue.
A saddle blanket here, or a hotel room there,
His back is as frail as is lacking his white hair.
Though the times were taking its toll on his ways,
He will continue to spread the Lords word throughout all of his days.

# The Meadow

We all looked forward to our meadow trip,
We made sure that we were good and didn't give our parents any lip.
This meadow is on Utah land,
The view is beautiful no matter where you stand.
The empty sheep pens give it that Old West feel,
You know that thousands of sheep had grazed on this meadow for real.
The blue sky, green grass and quietness of the moment make all troubles go away,
You could envision the sheep mowing down the delicious grass instead of hay.
An hour or two soaking up the environment of this special place,
Gives you the energy to put up with the rat race.

# The Mind

The mind is a warped thing,
Sometimes it forgets to ring.
It is suppose to remember who you are,
But it takes a break before it gets that far.
You are suppose to be at one place,
But usually more times than not that is not the case.
It also does not work to challenge your mind to a fight,
Because even if it is wrong it is right.
You try to fill it with facts,
When all along it hides what it lacks.
As you get older the rocks get larger and take up more space,
By then you are missing two many cylinders to race.

# The Mission

As the mortars were falling around him,
He felt that their chance of survival was slim.
There were eight of them this morning when they left the base,
To reach their objective they had to keep a steady pace.
They rode in a personnel carrier as far as they dared,
The Sergeant First Class for his squad's safety always cared.
Once on foot they stayed to the low country to not be seen,
They knew if they were detected to soon, things would get mean.
As they closed in on the enemy's camp they could see their light,
The Sergeant First Class directed his squad to the left and right.
They were calling in air support when a trip flare shown bright,
Mortars started falling close to their site.
The air support dropped their bombs and proved their worth,
The enemy's camp disappeared from its place on earth.
Eight men were healthy when they left on their mission that day,
With God on their side, they came back the same way.
Thousands of these missions are undertaken around the world every day,
By men and women who follow their superior's orders in every way.
These soldiers will protect the red, white and blue for all of time,
Their job is very serious, and their responsibility continues to climb.

# The Old Man

The old man sat there as the young kids acted up,
They reminded him of young unruly pups.
Their actions and words were not to his liking,
He remembers how quiet it was in the woods hiking.
The kids continued their antics until he could not stand them anymore,
He made an unfriendly remark that made them head for the door.
He knew the things he said were mean,
But then the words from the kids were not clean,
The old man was always irritated by the kids, who were arrogant and loud,
He remembers the kids from his era that were disciplined and proud.
The old man knows that he should not say those things,
Because of the trouble to him it could bring.
Parents always say that their child could never do wrong,
Even when they are behind bars for a time very long.
The old man continued to watch them play,
He would try next time to say something a different way.

# The P.A.L.M. Process

My husband had orders for war,
The thought of it shocked me to the core.
They say we have a P.A.L.M. tomorrow,
I am not sure what this is, mixed with my sorrow.
We arrived at 0700 hours,
I almost did not have time to shower.
The first item was for Larry to fill out a will,
Next was for me to know how to pay the bills.
Larry always handled the money,
Here; this is for the groceries honey.
They told me I had to write checks for all the bills,
I had never written a check and it gave me the chills.
Larry said; "How much money we had; I did not need to know",
Until now I had no idea about our cash flow.
My marriage was fine and I love my children so I was glad,
It was never important to me to know how much money we had.
After the P.A.L.M., I told myself that from now on,
I needed to know more about our finances for when Larry is gone.

# The Peaceful Valley

The sun sprang up over the mountain top,
The rabbit in the valley did hop.
The deer stood, stretched and checked on its newborn fawn,
The mountain goats eat the grass so it looked like a well maintained lawn.
The beavers play in the water as they build a dam,
The coyote looked up and saw the big horns of the ram.
The bear was stealing a meal from the honey bees,
The bald eagles were looking down from high in the trees.
The trout tried their best not to become a raccoon's feast,
The moose slowly walked in the reeds showing he is a majestic beast.
The squirrels chased after every nut,
While the bull elks faced off for their annual rut.
The snake slithered closer to his meal of a mouse,
Adding to the beauty of this valley is; there is not a house.
This valley has never been touched by man,
So nobody had ever changed the valley as part of their plan.
Life went on in the valley as it has done for years,
Without intervention by man there was not any reason for tears.
Hopefully this valley will never see broken sod,
As it is preserved the way it was created by God.

# The Peschongs

Peschong, Peschong, Peschong,
Ding Dong, Ding Dong, Ding Dong.
You can never believe what you hear,
They should be family of the year.
Go-Go Gertie is the mother,
She, with love her children smothers.
Many boys and girls did she bare,
As they grew, she did for them care.
The girls awarded her by taking other names,
They also tried to be tame, NOT.
Peschong is music to the ears,
But trying to spell it is difficult after too many beers.
Her children keep showing their love,
Always in ways that are beyond and above.
Though some of them are farther away than she wishes,
Some still live close enough to sometimes help with the dishes.
She is still very spry and with it,
Don't try to pull the wool over her eyes or give her any shit-zu.
Her family is her life,
Do not mess with her for she is handy with a knife.
I doubt if the part about the knife in the last phrase is true,
But it's the first thing that came to mind out of the blue.
I better close this poem before it gets too long,
I do not want to get in trouble for getting something wrong.

# The Phone

He sat by the phone for hours waiting for it to ring,
All he wanted was to hear the telephones sweet words sing.
He also walked back and forth until his feet hurt,
He was lucky though for the pain only came in spurts.
He was waiting for the call that would change his life,
It would make him very happy along with his wife,
He kicked at the floor as he looked at that thing,
It was silent as can be without even one ring.
The hours turned into days,
He thought of how he could destroy that phone in so many ways
He finally gave up on it coming alive,
He was ready to give up but instead he continued to strive.
The phone continues to be silent to him,
He cannot give up because it might ring on a whim.

# The Poker Hand

The tension at the poker table was amazing,
As the cards hit the table the fire in the players came out blazing.
The first two cards were dealt face down,
The look of anxiety on the player's faces could be seen all around.
The betting was furious before even seeing the "flop",
They started with eight players but then four of them did drop.
As the three "flop" cards hit the table the fans were aghast,
The cards showing made them anxious to see the "turn" and "river" that come last.
The four players left in the hand took their time to play,
I swear the hair on a couple of them turned a little gray.
The betting started slow but increased in a hurry,
By the lines on the player's faces they began to worry.
With the "turn" card face up on the table,
The four players left wondered if their brains were able.
This time the betting started out strong,
The intensity on the player's faces stated; what if I'm wrong?
The betting on the "turn" card finally came to a close,
Within the chests of the players their heart beats rose.
The dealer tapped the table, discarded two cards and let the "river" card fly,
As the image on the card hit the player's brains, you could see some of them want to cry.

Mostly their faces are very stoic,
When the cards fall just right, they even feel heroic.
The four players left in the hand looked at their cards and thought, should I bluff,
But with players of this caliber, bluffing is really tough.
The furious betting quickly put two more players on the side,
They quickly realized they'd only been along for the ride.
The final two players tried to read each other's eyes,
The tightness in their stomachs could be felt to their thighs.
Finally the betting was over for this hand,
It was time to see who is the best in the land.
As both player's hole cards were shown to all,
The player with the best hand imagined his picture on the winner's wall.

# The Slaughter House

The cows came down the chute a final time,
The door ahead displayed the fatal sign.
In the building they went single file,
To the other end of the line was not quite a mile.
The air hammer hit them hard in the head,
The cold cement floor was their death bed.
They were hung up and started down the line,
At the end they will be covered with a cloth soaked in salt brine.
The workers on the line were quick with their tools,
To ensure the best quality meat they followed the rules.
They were cut and sliced until their hide came off easy,
If you are not used to seeing this, your stomach might get queasy.
Their entrails were pulled out onto a conveyor belt,
They put them into a machine where they became tripe after the melt.
They are inspected and stamped for the quality they should meet,
They are stored in the freezer after being covered with the salt brine sheet.
It was a test of your stomach when they stopped for lunch,
They ate in the lunch room as one bunch.
Their hands were covered with cow juice,
A sight that can make some peoples stomachs loose.

# The Song

The room resembled a recycle yard,
It was all sheets of crumpled paper and a few birthday cards.
I have been trying to write this song forever,
I feel like the finished product will be never.
The first verse came to him very fast,
Getting the second and third verses right felt like they would be his last.
He played the versus over and over in his mind,
But he couldn't come up with a chorus of any kind.
After two weeks and two bottles of gin,
He finally came up with something that could win.
He turned the song over to a friend for the music to write,
He felt good knowing the end of the song was in sight.
Six months from the day that he started the song,
It went number one and now nothing could go wrong.

# The Stalker

Her desire to always be with him is strong,
She said her time with him would be long.
She first saw him years ago,
At which time her self-esteem was low.
She sent him letters and emails every day,
She knew she needed to be with him in every way.
Her walls were covered with his pictures ceiling to floor,
In her closet were boxes with many more.
She worshiped the ground that he walked on,
She could not fathom the fact that he was from her gone.
She spent all her money following him on trips,
She took thousands of video clips.
Her obsession got to the point after time,
That stealing his things; to her was not a crime.
The day she bought the gun,
She had made up her mind that he could no longer run.
If they could not be together here,
Then she was ready to kill him and herself without any fear.
The day the police found them laying side by side,
They knew that for both of them, this was the end of their ride.

# The Stripper

Her muscles tensed as she stood behind the curtain,
When the music started she knew what she had to do for certain.
This was not her first choice for work,
She came across it on a quirk.
As she came through the curtain she became another body,
Her gyrations brought whistles and hollering because she was a hottie.
As she moved her breasts swelled and her hips moved left and right,
The men stared like they had not seen a better sight.
As her breasts separated from her bra, she wondered what her mother would think,
This action was necessary for the men to buy a drink.
She was relieved when the music stopped and her dance was over,
Her mind wondered back to her mother living in Dover.
When you are a stripper, all men think you can be had very easy,
Most men who want to bed down a stripper are usually sleazy.
She took this job because it was good money,
She gets sick to her stomach when the men call her honey.
She attend college full time to eventually get ahead,
She did not want to get in just any man's bed.
With this job the hours are short and the money is big,
This gave her extra time for her studies and math course in Trig.
As she heads for work tonight, she knew this is what had to be,
She could also use the mental part for her degree in Psychology.

# The Suit from Hell

Going to work each day should be fun,
It is not fun to wear a black suit in the sun.
The days when the temperature is 110,
When the shift is done, you are glad it is now instead of then.
As you dress for work you feel the tightness of the tie,
This feels like in the Old West when they hung'em high.
Your black suit coat hangs in the car,
It laughs at you knowing you have to wear it in a time not too far.
You watch the weather hoping for cooler times,
When you see nothing but triple digits, you scream "This is a crime."
When you get to work, you say why,
"Can't the weather person just one time lie?".
As I put on my black suit coat the sun burns the material into my back,
It did not help to think of laying on a big ice sack.
I grit my teeth and walk quickly to the room,
In there the smell of a hot iron does loom.
When you have to outside go,
You hope that you duties are not slow.
Ten seconds in the sun, the heat can be felt,
You cuss as you feel like you are going to melt.
Dress shoes or high heels make your feet hurt,
The ladies have it worse when they have to wear a skirt.
You know you do not have a choice on what to wear,
You wish that headquarters would a little more care.
You will continue to wear the black suit because you need to work,
Bill collectors always in the bushes lurk.

# The Troll

They were told that the house was strange,
To be safe they should stay out of range.
They said that nothing could scare them at all,
The night they decided to go; it was coming on fall.
They broke the latch and proceeded in,
They knew this would be an easy bet to win.
What they did not know is the danger within this house,
Before the night was over they would know it was not a mouse.
There was a flesh eating Troll behind the wall they started to disassemble,
When he finished devouring them, a human they will not resemble.
On one side they slowly removed the planks,
On the other side the Troll was salivating thinking of their tasty shanks.
He sat quietly trying to control himself before the meal,
As they removed the last plank, they laughed and said "This is no deal.".
Before they could move, the Troll ripped off some of their parts,
If they had lived long enough they would have said it smarts.
When the police found their parts they could not believe their sight,
The way they were ripped a part was just not right.
They never did figure out what happened to the two,
They buried the parts of the two men but could not find their shoes.
The house was closed up again and hopefully left alone for good,
The troll waited behind a different wall of wood.

# The Wagon Train

The twenty wagons left Denver on the first of May,
Reverend Law was the wagon master on that fateful day.
The mountains just west of Denver made their going slow,
The horses and oxen were not the best and didn't want to go.
Reverend Law slightly remembers anything about the sale,
It was after he left the saloon and almost got run out of town on a rail.
When he awoke in the middle of the corral at first light,
The strange beasts around him looked quite a sight.
After fast talking his way out of a noose,
He decided he better keep his guns pretty loose.
Staying to the low areas of the mountains,
Made the mile high waterfalls look like beautiful fountains.
Reverend Law's memory was good considering his many lost brain cells,
But it was still amazing that he remembered all the water wells.
The trip to reach their new homes was hard for all,
Sober again, Reverend Law was sure they could reach Genoa, Nevada by fall.
Traveling through the mountains was a beautiful sight,
Soon the families knew that Reverend Law was for the Wagon Master right.
By July they had from Colorado to Utah strained,
Also by this time the horses and oxen to the trail were well trained.
The beauty of Utah even surpassed the Colorado valleys,

The Utah terrain and the steeper route made the livestock have to rally.
Years of wagon trains using the same way had worn down the trail,
This is the same trail that will be used later by the Pony Express to deliver mail.
Reverend Law pushed the wagon train on through sun and rain as they go,
With the biggest and hardest challenges being the few rivers rapid flow.
It took precious time for them to find a way around the Great Salt Lake,
Into present day Nevada then part of Utah Territory did Reverend Law them take.
They also had to face the Western Shoshone Indians whose land they had to cross,
When they came upon a Western Shoshone camp, their words were at a loss.
Reverend Law was able to explain that they would not permanently stop,
The children played along the wagons as they over the sagebrush did hop.
The 18 valleys and 10 mountain passes across Nevada did take their toll,
They left behind 24 shallow graves when they finally into Genoa roll.
Of the 90 that started Paiute Indians and accidents caused those 24,
If it was not for Reverend Law there would have been a lot more.
They were able to build shelter and gather food as winter was on its way,
Many of their generations still live in Genoa to this very day.

# The Wind

The wind was calm early in the day,
The animals were out playing many different ways.
A chipmunk (not Alvin) jumped into the air,
The wind came up and bounced him off the bear.
From nowhere the wind was blowing strong,
All the animals ran for cover not knowing what was wrong.
The squirrels ran for their hole in the tree,
Once there they jumped up and down with glee.
The poor birds were trying to fly west,
They were not getting anywhere even trying their best.
A mouse came flying through the air just missing the cat.
Next being pushed along were many bats.
The wind got stronger as the night went on,
If this keeps up the whole forest will be gone.
All of a sudden it was calm; all the animals looked around,
The ones that could, ran into burrows in the ground.
The tornado they expected did not come their way,
They are all thankful for this day.
The wind was calm early in the day,
The animals were out playing many different ways.

# This Lady is Good

I know a lady who is smart,
She will research something from the start.
This story is true to the facts,
New cars she researches to the max.
When to the dealer she did go,
The salesman saw the lady and said HO HO HO.
She told him what she wanted for a car,
The salesman thought he had an easy sale, before heading to the bar.
She stopped him in his tracks when he said this or that,
When she corrected him so many times, he wanted to hide under his hat.
He said this can be added very easy,
She knew he was wrong and felt he was sleazy.
He tried to sell her a car for more money,
She said "First of all sleaze bag, I am not your honey".
She left that day with the car she wanted at a lower price,
The salesman was hauled away mumbling something about giant mice.

# Those Few Seconds

The cancer had taken its toll,
In a few minutes it will reach its goal.
He had heard about the last few seconds before death,
Then there will be quiet and eternal rest.
Suddenly the pain was gone and he was in a field of grain,
Everything was quiet and serene and coming from outside his brain.
He could see friends and relative from his past,
He knew now that everything from the living world he had seen last.
Now he was floating towards a bright light,
When he got to it, there was quite a sight.
He saw God along with many people gathered around him in his old Ford,
He knew now that he had lived a good life and eternity was his reward.

# Three Chihuahuas by Cosmo

I was fortunate to become a member of the Weaver family home,
They are so loving and caring that I will never have to roam.
Then I had a brother and a sister with which to play,
Our dad and mom made sure we did not stray.
We grew up in Ely, Nevada having a lot of fun,
Dad and mom made sure we had plenty of room to run.
We were the Three Chihuahuas so we did not need a lot of space,
We used to run around the house and yard like we were in a race.
We all three met Uncle Dan and Aunt Sandy sometime along the way,
They treat us good and spoil us; it was our lucky day.
Mom left one day and did not come back,
We did not see her leave for we were asleep on the sack.
We were confused at first but dad was there to keep us safe every day,
Later we had a different mom who we love very much and glad she stayed.
As Takita and I got older, it was harder with Gidget to play,
We could not run faster or longer like yesterday.
Takita and I are almost 14 years old now,
We both have enjoyed life as much as we know how.
I have been feeling poorly lately and I hurt some times,
Dad looks so funny when he teases mom, he looks like a mime.
Aunt Sandy is here to take the Three Chihuahuas for a ride,

I cannot get up and stay with Takita and Gidgets strides.
We are at Uncle Dan and Aunt Sandy's house now,
I am feeling really bad; I wish I was feeling better but I do not know how.
If I go to dog heaven without making it through the night,
I want dad and mom to know I loved my life and they did it right.
I am feeling worse as my eyes will not focus and my chest feels real tight,
I will always be in their hearts and they have my two poems to be in their sight.
They still have Takita and Gidget to love as they loved me,
There will now be Two Chihuahuas but I will be watching from above; you see.
I cannot forget Aunt Sandy, who treated us like her own,
Or Uncle Dan who held me and stayed with me as I traveled to my new home.

# Thrill of the Kill

He silently in the shadows stayed,
He could smell her scent and was not dismayed.
As she came into sight he started to shake,
He knew he had to be fast before her fingernails could rake.
His quickness was on the mark,
The knife bit in like a great white shark.
She died without taking another step,
He knew the newspapers would continue to build his rep.
The thrill of the kill sent shivers to his core,
He knew his time was short and what was in store.
The urge in him to kill was strong,
In his warped way he didn't think it was wrong.
It didn't matter to him whether it was a woman or a man,
All he knew is that he has to kill whoever he can.
The first kill caught him by surprise,
But each kill after gave him a bigger rise.
He knew to keep killing he had to increase the speed,
Especially with the FBI on his trail with Reed.
He decided after the last kill he would stop this his way,
Which he did with his own knife on his selected day.
After his death the FBI felt like he was the one,
They believed he had done it for fun.
As he looked up from the fires of hell,
He know that the families would never have closure; Oh Well!!

# Tim and Anna

Their names are Tim and Anna Curtin,
There is one thing for certain.
Two nicer people you won't find,
Looking right, left, front or behind.
Their spiritual faith is their guiding light,
Their mission in life is to do all that is right.
On an Alaskan cruise they did go,
It didn't matter how much the dough.
The cruise was very enjoyable and a lot of fun,
Even though the seas, made some for the pills run.
Twenty-Four/Seven enticed by beverage and food,
Treated like a King and Queen, puts all in the best mood.
The beauty of the sea and the shoreline are real,
Which made this cruise, no matter the cost, the best deal.
Back at home their beloved cats are watched over by son Royce,
Whose counting the days until they return home, rejoice.
After the cruise they visited loved ones in Washington State,
Their three grandchildren to whom they can almost always relate.
This poem is a gift for two very special friends,
Who are always there for us, right now or just around the bend.
We are glad that you made it home safe and sound,
Even though the cruise might possibly have made you a little more round.

# Timothy Paul Curtin's Retirement

To cover the life of Timothy P. Curtin,
You have to cover five areas; for certain.
Area One is his early life in a few lines,
To start this Poem of Timothy and his times.
As a young man growing up in Washington, D. C.,
The Nuns in the school prayed that his graduation was soon to be.
With tears of joy in their eyes and arms moving all wavy,
The Nuns gleefully shipped him off to the Navy.

Area Two covers some of his Navy career of over twenty-three years,
A few of his assignments also included X amount of beers.
The Navy was the life that was his to be,
He excelled in everything on land and sea.
His destiny was to serve his country in Viet Nam times three,
Where as a Seabee he used his exceptional skills to keep people free.
Most people select enlisted, warrant officer or commissioned officer for their rank,
But all three did Timothy achieve, a rarity you can take to the bank.
Some of his assignments were very vital to his countries freedom,
Moving information that only at the highest level could readem.
As a Lieutenant Commander he retired from the Navy,
He decided as a teacher he could still bring home some more gravy.

Area Three covers his life for the next seventeen years,
As a teacher in Ely, Nevada, and fewer number of beers.
His natural personality was a hit with all the students in Ely,
If you have any doubts you can ask the students, really.
The pictures on the White Pine County High School wall,
Show Tim with a lot more hair before it started to fall.
From teacher to Vice Principal to Assistant Superintendent he did achieve.
Until he decided to retire again to Las Vegas would you believe.

Area Four covers the timeframe from Ely up to today,
Where we all are blessed with what we get to say.
His move to Las Vegas would not slow him down,
At first he had to learn a lot about this new town.
When asked to start a new school for SEAS Parish,
He knew this was a request that he would always cherish.
The curriculum, the staff, the colors, the dress code,
He ensured that everything was starting in the right mode.
The School has progressed to where he is leaving it today,
Accreditation and outstanding staff will keep it that way.
As he changes his lifestyle once again and removes items from his office walls,
His legacy will always be felt as we continue to walk the halls.

Area Five of his life is the most important one of all,
It is his Family and Faith in God; both which makes him stand tall.
One day long ago in California his heart skipped a beat,
As he eyed a beautiful woman in the CA heat.
Anna Mariani from Ely, Nevada is her name,
God's intervention intended for her to Tim tame.
Their marriage was a perfect match because both of them give,
To this day their love and caring for each other still lives.
Twin boys; Rex and Royce, by God, they were given one day,
Into outstanding professional men they grew in their own way.
In the Philippines, Romania and other places she was by his side,
Learning to live in many environments sometimes was quite a ride.
This also included many times when Anna and the boys stayed behind,
As Tim served his country sometimes with attire of different kinds.
Close together or far apart their Love and Faith did never wain,
In fact, after all these years their Love and Faith in God has grown no matter sun or rain.
Just mention their grandchildren if you want to see a smile on their face,
They cherish every minute they can spend with them, no matter the place.
As Tim moves on to another phase in his life, all we can say,
Is Thank you; as your family and faith continue to guide your way.

(This poem is dedicated to my good friend Timothy P. Curtin.)

# To Walk or Not

We have lived our lives by the golden rules,
That does not mean that we have been fools.
We have always paid our bills,
But lately trying to pay them is giving us chills.
Having been laid-off from my job,
Makes us both feel like our souls have been robbed.
After a year of struggling to survive,
Time for our final decision has arrived.
All people in the know tell us the same thing to do,
We have to stop paying our mortgage in order to start new.
The programs the government have, are supposed to help,
They fail to do this while taking your scalp.
The current foreclosure alternative program sounds good,
But behind it is a feeling of a person with a gun wearing a hood.
After discussing our choices we will do what we must,
If we wait too long we will be covered with rust.

# Tony and Connie Soliz

Tony and Connie were sweethearts,
They knew they were meant for each other from the start.
From New Mexico's Spanish heritage they came,
One thing for sure their love for each other was not a game.
The U.S. Army was Tony's career to be,
They moved around for the next twenty years you see.
During this time they brought two beautiful daughters into their life,
Connie raised them when Tony was away; as is the life of an Army wife.
When the Army for them was through,
They retired to Silver City, New Mexico and its good old brew.
The two daughters now grown and Tony and Connie with grandchildren on their lap,
They knew he was an easy mark as with any grandma and grandpap.
Some health problems for Connie came along the way,
But their prayers and faith in the Lord keep them going every day.
Tony continues to help his military comrades by working for the VA for one and all,
He helps them receive their benefits after they have hit a wall.
They have always had a strong faith in the Lord,
He should let them in the pearly gates even if their still driving that old Bronco Ford.

# Training a New Officer

Assigned to train a new officer can be a chore,
New officers are nervous and might faint to the floor.
You can explain things to them many times,
But to them you are talking in rhymes.
There are a lot of things for them to learn,
The Rules and Procedures give them a lot of concern.
The Post Orders add even more for them to remember,
Their main concern is to still be here past December.
These are the posts where officers have to work,
All of them having different duties that can be full of quirks.
For the Main Gate officer, the visitor has to be valid,
Oh, Oh, I forgot to bring my lunch of salad.
The Patrol officer must learn this difficult place,
With hourly checks sometimes they have to race.
The Lobby officer has to always be on the ball,
They have to be 100% on the elevators they call.
All of the new officers normally do pretty well,
But they will not be there long if they use their cell.
When a veteran officer hears they will be a trainer,
They hope that afterwards their brain will be saner.
If you see a person in a dark suit praying on their knees,
It is a trainer hoping that the trainee did not lose the keys.
The trainers always worry about their hair when their name is called,
Most of them keep their hair cut close so they already look bald.

# Tranquility

The remembrance is like yesterday in my mind,
I do not think there is another calming effect of any kind.
It was me, a red Farmall A tractor with mower and forty acres of alfalfa field,
The alfalfa was very thick and should have a high yield.
In that field the rest of the world did not exist,
The only issue is if the heavy alfalfa does the mower blade resist.
The alfalfa makes a beautiful sight as it falls behind the mower cut,
Sometimes the barn yard dog came with; the mangy mutt.
You start with the mower blade next to the fence,
Then you reverse and cut inward forth hence.
You cut one side then make a circle to cut another side,
The Farmall A tractor is small and bumpy to ride.
Each cut of a side makes the field smaller,
It is relaxing because nobody can hear you even if you holler.
The day is done and so is the mowed field looking so bare,
When I get back to the farm house I am going to ride the mare.
There is no better feeling than just you and the earth,
These chances do not come often so remember them for all they are worth.

# Tribute to Tobie (Golden Retriever)

Tobie was my name,
Giving love and companionship was my game.
My life with David, Terry and Dominic was the best,
For many years until it was time for my final rest.
My life was full of fun and play,
From my time as a puppy, until my final day.
To Dominic; my brother and my best friend,
Our years together were the best ever to the end.
To Terry, my mother who watched over me 24/7,
You know God is now watching over me in Heaven.
To David, my father; who kept us all safe,
Your gentle touch helped my transition to a lovely place.
I am now gone from my place next to the hearth,
But I will always be with each of you in your heart.

# Trip to Italy

This poem is for Tim and Anna Curtin,
There is one thing for certain.
A happier more deserving couple you won't find,
For the lucky people who know them, the two make one of a kind.
Off to Italy for a much needed vacation they did roam,
Boy, by the world map that is sure a long ways from home.
Anna was happy again to use her Italian tongue,
Tim on the other hand tried to use his Italian without being hung.
Their Italian relatives where always cordial and kind,
But you had to keep on your toes to not get left behind.
Down this road and up that mountain they did go,
Is that tree wide enough for the nature stop, oh oh?
The food in Italy was so good; what was that they just ate,
Who cares; it was really great, now the problem is my weight.
The tears did run when they left for home, but none of them did whine,
Until they got to the Rome airport and saw that long, long line.
Around four hours later their scheduled flight did depart,
Boy, the joy of this modern traveling is hard on the heart.
Home again, home again merrily they did go; and then they say,
Rome, Newark, Houston all in what seemed like one long, long day.
Finally in Summerlin they did arrive with only one thought; to heal,
Hooly, Mooly Miss Anna, 115 degrees is HOT, this ain't no deal.

# True Friends

No better friends can you find,
Than those that put you at peace of mind,
Gary and Sandy are their names,
Friendship for them is real and not a game,
When you need a friend with whom to talk;
You can count on them never to walk,
Their sense of humor is the best,
For they put up with us not like some of the rest,
They make life here in Ely,
A joy for us believe me; really.

# Trust

A five letter word that controls earth,
People depend on this word for all they are worth.
From birth people must believe in it,
Lack of this word has caused many to quit.
This word has stopped wars,
But when broken it can leave sores.
This word is required most in a personal relationship between two,
Love is held together with this word being the glue.
This word can create happiness and sustain it for life,
Especially in a relationship between a husband and wife.
Too many people jump to a conclusion to fast in relation to this word,
They do not research the facts but go by what they have heard.
The bottom line is you go through life with or without this word as part of you,
You must decide how this word affects you and then do what you must do.
You can never let this word rust,
When the word you are talking about is TRUST.

# Turning Fifty

Turning fifty is quite nifty for Sandy,
Who is still cute as a button and very dandy.
Born to the family of Wayne and Bernadine Strand,
This family has always been a number one brand.
She was raised in a small town named Randall,
Knowing right from wrong, she never flew off the handle.
She married a young man named Dan Noss,
Whose love and affection for her is never at a lose.
She has traveled the world to follow her husband's career,
Has supported him whether the Army took him far or near.
No human children were desired by both and medically this came to pass,
But many dogs and cats throughout the years gave them lots of joy to last.
Currently with names of Sadie, Brittnee, Milo and Mandy,
These children (pets) give additional love and joy to the life of Sandy.
Almost thirty-two years have passed since her marriage in May,
To both Dan and Sandy Noss this is still a very special day.
As gracefully as her fiftieth birthday approaches near and near,
Her family, friends and husband wish her the best for the rest of her years.
This birthday poem is from her husband Dan,
Who is happy everyday that she picked him for her man.

# Two Illinois Ladies

Two beautiful ladies from Illinois to Las Vegas came,
Hoping to win a Megajackpot was their game.
Wanda and Vivian are their names,
Their names were changed to protect the guilty; just the same.
They checked out some entertainment during the night,
Boy; those Chippendale dancers are sssoooo right.
Their tour guide, E. P. made them like little school girls giggle,
Especially when he gave them that famous wiggle.
Those silk polka dot sleep pants about said it all,
Thank God they didn't decide to fall.
They left the freezing Illinois snow,
To bask in the Las Vegas sun and take in a show.
The weather turned out to be a pain,
Good old Las Vegas clouds, cold and rain.
Their host Susan made their time in Las Vegas the best,
Susan told them when you get back to the frozen north, you can rest.
They didn't win the Megajackpot but their time in Las Vegas was still great,
They were both happy to be going back to Illinois and to their mates.
When they got back home their feet were sore,
The last thing they can say about their trip is that it was not a bore.

# Two Massacres

The scout laying flat on top of the hill,
Could see the Sioux village in the morning chill.
The Indians were starting to move around,
He had to get back to the detachment without making a sound.
He reported to his Commander how many Indians were there,
The Commander took in the information with an evil stare.
There were about 50 women and children in the camp,
The Commander devised his attack by the light of the lamp.
The warriors were away hunting on a one week trip,
The soldiers would have to quietly into the camp slip.
Without warning they started firing at all,
The women and children did quickly fall.
At the fort the Commander reported that all the warriors had died,
He knew that nobody would question if he had lied.
The warriors returned to find their women and children were all dead,
They followed the soldiers intending to fill them full of lead.
The next day the Commander and his detachment left on patrol,
The Commander was confident and of his men he knew he was in control.
The warriors lay in wait to make them pay,
They planned to leave the soldiers where they lay.

Their attack was swift and effective,
They were not very selective.
The Commander was the last to die as he cried for his life,
At this point he was sorry he had started this strife.
The warriors made his death torturous and slow,
The sparkle in his eyes would never again glow.
This tit for tat went back and forth,
From the South to the North.
The soldiers kept coming as the Indians grew less,
The Indians tried and tried but ended up in a mess.
Eventually their freedom to roam was gone,
They were expected to live in a house with a lawn.
For the Indians the writing was on the wall,
Their lifestyle was gone but they could still hold their heads up tall.
The Indians devastation has been played out in movies and books for years,
That has left them with a wide river of tears.

# Two Shots

He looked through the scope and saw them both there,
To his dismay, clothes they did not wear.
One was his lover and the other was his wife,
The anger boiled in him as he decided to take their lives.
He kept thinking about which one to take out first,
He knows that the one that is last will feel the anguish worse.
He decided his wife would be the first to go,
Seeing her laying in a pool of blood would excite him to his toes.
His Lover would be more likely to stay with him than her,
As the shot shattered her spine everything to him seemed a blur.
She fell forward and to the right,
Even for him it was not a pretty sight.
His lover jumped up with horror,
He could see that his lover was shakin' to the core.
The next shot went straight through his lover's left eye,
He calmly set down the rifle and slapped at a fly.
Deep inside himself he started to cheer,
Then on his face came a leer.
At the last second he decided to kill his lover to,
That way if his lover decided he could not sue.
He sat back and waited for the police to come that day,
But at least he would go out his own way.

# Uncle and Niece

There is a young lady named Jessica from Longview,
Who has an uncle; to see she had no clue.
Jessica grew into a beautiful woman with unforgettable looks,
The first time they had seen each other's picture was on Facebook.
They corresponded a few lines,
It was good for both of them at the time.
She was married in August 2010,
She sent out invitations early so he would know when.
He put it on his calendar and looked forward to go,
He was laid-off which changed all his plans though.
He was hoping the wedding to make,
It ended up he couldn't make it which made his heart break.
He was so looking forward to meeting her this summer,
The turns that life gives you is sometimes a bummer.
He wants to ask for her forgiveness for missing her wedding,
If there are some pictures to see, he can look at the spectacular setting.
If there was any way he could have been there,
He would have showed up because he cares.
Hopefully in the future they will be able to meet together,
If their luck doesn't change, that meeting will probably be delayed by the weather.

# Vegas Anger

Vegas sucks,
When you do not have any luck.
You try to win big,
What a sorry gig.
If you spend too much time on the strip,
You will be more screwed on this trip.
They entice you with free booze,
Once drunk, you will more lose.
No back streets for you,
Unless you want the funeral thing to do.
They will strip you of your clothes,
Then cut off your moles.
On Freemont Street you must stay,
Ogden or Stewart, you better pray.
The glitz and glitter are fine for some,
To others it seems pretty dumb.
Between the rich and the poor is a big spread,
The poor are always in the red.
In Vegas do not answer unless asked,
Do not ask questions without wearing a mask.
Politian's in Nevada are the worst,
Underhanded politics in Las Vegas are always in first.
The gangs from California keep moving in,
Why can't they stay in California and keep the crime within.
This poem has some anger in it,
When you think of Las Vegas it can give you a fit.
My apologies to the Mayor of Las Vegas who does care,
There are some good things about Las Vegas if you do not live there.

# White Man's Point of View

We fought for this land and purchased the rest,
We can go anywhere and do what we do best.
If there is gold in those hills,
We can go get it as we will.
I can also kill all the buffalo we want any day,
There are so many they will never go away.
I do not want the meat and bones and it saves on hay,
The tongue and the hide are the only things that pay.
I heard of gold farther west so I will move there,
It is Indian land but the soldiers will protect me so I do not care.
I did not personally sign the treaty so it does not pertain to me,
Indians do not mean anything to me; I will just shoot them if they ask for a fee.
I have an idea for all Indians; force them on to a small piece of ground,
Then I can steal and pillage from their land when nobody else is around.
We can make them farmers against their will,
Make them work hard for the field to till.
We will make them depend on us,
Tell them more lies when they make a fuss.
We will call this land a reservation,
Punish them if they leave to go back to their Indian nation.
If we keep them there forever,
We can make sure they are powerful again, never.

# Who Is She

She is still beautiful to this day,
She is strong and has learned how to do it her way.
She raised four children, who turned out good,
With a little help from a paddle made of wood.
They all entered into marriage at even spaces,
Some of their childhood toys and memories were the only traces.
With spouses and children of their own,
The chances are far and few between to visit her home.
She lost her husband and love in the month of September,
Her heart still aches when she thinks of him and remembers.
She always was handy at many things,
Doing some of them every day great joy brings.
She still cuts her grass with a push lawn mower,
When it comes to flowers she is a heck of a grower.
Though she is getting up in the years,
Thoughts of the loss of her husband still brings tears.
One day she hired a young man, who to her house came,
She helped him clean up the large yard and put him to shame.
She had problems with her body that created a lot of pain,
This feeling in her body intensified when it rained.
She shines with joy when her children and their families stop by,
After they leave she thinks about how infrequent their visits are and why.
She knows they have lives of their own,
That they are only as far away as a phone.
To hear their voice is good for her heart,
Then she remembers how loud they used to fart.
She cooked; I mean kept the books for many clubs,
But do not worry she used her own money for the massage rubs.
This poem could go on forever about her life,
She is a mother, grandmother, great-grandmother and widowed wife.
But it is time to find out who is leader of her band,
She is no other than Bernadine Strand.

# Who Is The Poor Man

The poor man sat on the side,
The rich man showed off his ride.
The poor man did not know his next meal,
The rich man had so many cars it didn't seem real.
The poor man had holes in his shoes,
The rich man laughed when told to follow the rules.
The poor man struggled to keep what he had,
The rich man complained about the size of his pad.
The poor man went home to a happy family with joy,
The rich man went home to an unhappy family without joy.
The poor man's love within his family made him rich,
The rich man's lack of love within his family made him poor.
This poems true meaning can cut some people like a knife,
True happiness comes out of love, not money throughout life.

# Why Me

In the last month my luck was not to be,
Three vehicles have hit the gate; why can't they see.
They notice the bar when they pull up and stop,
I verify their entrance then their brain must skip and hop.
Every time; I turned to raise the bar when they started to move,
The last time I hollered but he had already the paint grooved.
They all backed up but did not get out and look,
They did not have a scratch or dent like what can be made by a hook.
Just a little white paint from the bar,
Their grills were OK on their car.
It never pays to be in a hurry,
Because most times you end up having to worry.
Will they have to pay to get it fixed?,
At this point the decision is mixed.

# Work Environment

Coming to work each day should be fun,
Some supervisors want to put you under the gun.
They usually seem mad from the days start,
They really holler if they hear you fart.
They say do this or do not do that,
Either way they make you feel like you are a rat.
It does not matter that you have not been given the information,
They expect you to know everything for your station.
When they settle down as the day goes on,
They make working fun for a few minutes before you are home gone.

# Working for the Rich

Working for the rich can be a nightmare for many,
Some of them act like they never had to live on pennies.
When you try to interpret their thoughts,
You will always be wrong and get caught.
You try to use common sense when they want something,
Trouble to yourself and others is all you will bring.
When they live in a million dollar condo they can be prudes,
They also do not have any problems being rude.
All we can do is wish that they lose everything they got,
Then they will have to cook a soup stone in a pot.

# The End

This is the end of my first book,
I hope that you have enjoyed this look.
I started writing poems for friends one day,
Later I decided to expand the topic areas in many ways.
I named the book *Poems of Everyday Life,*
My goal was for a moment to take you away from any strife.
It felt good in my heart to write some poems to help my friends sorrow,
Other poems might seem out of place today, but who knows about tomorrow.

*Danny L. Noss*

Danny L. Noss